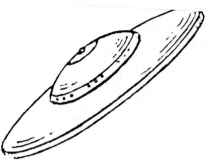

THE

AMERICAN INDIAN —

UFO STARSEED

CONNECTION

INNER LIGHT PUBLICATIONS

Editorial Direction & Layout
Timothy Green Beckley

Manuscript Production
Soltec Publishing Services

Published by:
INNER LIGHT PUBLICATIONS
P.O. BOX 753
NEW BRUNSWICK, N.J. 08903
Current book catalog sent free upon request.

ISBN
0-938294-90-3

COVER ART BY: JIM DALLMEIER

CONTENTS

Title	Page
AMERICAN INDIANS: HOW DO THEY FIT INTO THE UFO PUZZLE?	5
AMERICAN INDIANS AND THE STAR PEOPLE	9
SECRETS OF THE TOTEM	20
PLAYGROUND OF THE GODS	26
STAR GODS, HOPI REVELATIONS AND THE MISSING SACRED STONE	35
DO HOPI PROPHECIES HOLD KEY TO MYSTERIOUS ARTIFACT?	46
HOW THE INDIANS CONTACT UFO INTELLIGENCE THROUGH DREAMS	49
STRANGERS FROM ANOTHER WORLD	56
THE KACHINAS—REPRESENTATIVES OF THE GODS	61
KASSKARA—THE LOST PARADISE	66
CONTACT IN HOPILAND	80
SIGHTINGS OF BIGFOOT REVIVE HOPI LEGEND OF TRIBAL GOD	85
UFO STORIES OF THE NORTHWESTERN INDIANS	88
CULTIVATING THE STARSEED CONNECTION	93
VISION AT COURTHOUSE ROCK, SEDONA, ARIZONA	104

AMERICAN INDIANS: HOW DO THEY FIT INTO THE UFO PUZZLE?

The author of this chapter, Diane Tessman, is a rather unique individual. First, she is one of the few female UFO researchers/writers to have covered the subject for any length of time and second, a good measure of her material is strikingly intuitive as she is a full fledged channel. Her space contact, Tibus, is responsible for some fascinating cosmic discourses, and her encounters have been verified by Ruth Montgomery who wrote about her in the best-selling *Aliens Among Us*, and by Dr. Leo Sprinkle, formerly associated with the University of Wyoming. In this opening chapter, Diane reveals the link between Amerindians and the UFO puzzle. Ms. Tessman can be reached directly at Box 1, Callan, Kilkenny, Ireland.

I am in this world
I travel in the air
I was not born in the earth
I was born in the sky
My father is the North Cloud
My mother, the South Cloud

I will come to call you from the ocean
You will be needed in this world
When the trees come, you will
quicken them
When people come, you will comfort
them
You will make the life of the people
Do not refuse me
I am not deceiving you
  from ANNIKADEL by C. Hart Merriman

The above poem reflects the mystical quality which has always existed in the American Indians' way of living. And beyond that, it strongly suggests that American Indians have had on-going contact with Space Intelligences. In fact, one might read this poem as a message from a space brother or sister, being given to an enlightened human down on Earth. Indeed, it is similar to many of the transmissions being received regularly by space channels and star people, sent from UFO beings high above Earth in orbiting craft.

Just how do the American Indians' spiritual gifts and mystical experiences fit into the general UFO phenomenon and the specific field of contact with the occupants of UFOs?

The key to these questions lies in the fact that the American Indian practices a very advanced form of mysticism. The Indian reality blends the mystical and the logical into a way of thinking, living, feeling, and being. In the past, this was even more dynamic than it is today because the Indian ways have faded as the white man's religion continues to invade the Indian's world.

Most people feel that UFO beings are highly advanced in the fields of technology. Obviously this is true. One has only to sight a UFO zooming through the sky at tremendous speeds, doing impossible maneuvers to realize this. However, what most people do not take into consideration is that UFO beings are also very advanced spiritually. They are highly mystical beings with power of telepathy, healing, prophesy, and other paranormal abilities. It is easier to contact these UFO beings through advanced psychic abilities that it is to build a space ship and contact them through highly advanced technology.

In other words, no one on Earth has been able to build starships which equal UFOs in speed, agility, and ability to travel great universal distances. However, a few people on Earth do have the mystical knowledge and telepathic gifts to reach the UFO beings through advanced paranormal means. This is humanity's "best bet" for contact with space brothers and sisters, especially when these UFO beings also send messages, with the great hope that a human somewhere will hear it. Therefore, one might not have to reach telepathically all the way to the starship, because the Space intelligences are searching all the time, sending telepathic messages to Earth. These messages are as near as the air you breathe and the sunshine in which you walk.

Now we can see how the American Indian, with advanced mystical abilities, has been contacted so much throughout the years. The entire Indian lifestyle is (or used to be) designed around nature. The Indians do not distinguish between nature down on Earth and the cosmic energies out in space, while the white man tends to separate nature as being on Earth only and "space" as being a totally separate concept, when in fact, nature is cosmic energy personified within a planet's atmosphere. The wisdom that the American Indian possesses in his daily lifestyle is great. Until the interference of the white man, the Indian lived in total harmony with nature and universal energies. In fact the Indian is/was one with nature. . . part of it as surely as the owl, the oak tree, the moon and the stars.

In researching the UFO mystery, this nature connection has been overlooked by scientists and skeptics. Mysticism is not valued as important or even a valid reality. Yet American Indians have lived as mystical beings for thousands of years and, in doing so, have encountered many other forms of life, from Earth and beyond.

One group of humans who realize how important this mystical connection is are the Star People. Therefore, the Star People also feel a strong sense of identity with the American Indian. Of the thousands of letters I have received from Star People and UFO contactees throughout the years, about three fourths of these letters expressed the feeling that the writer has lived a past life as an American Indian, or that the writer has studied American Indian ways and spent time in Indian country or with Indians. I have been told that in a past life I lived as an Apache; as a child, I always played in my "Indian

by Dr. Diane Tessman,

7

stronghold" (there were no attacking cowboys. I simply imagined a very natural Indian life). In the letters I have received, individuals have mentioned their strong feelings of other past lives in France, China, Peru, Atlantis, England, etc., but there is no other singular experience which is mentioned more often than the American Indian experience! If a Star Person drives through Indian land, he or she will invariably feel something strange, powerful, and very natural. The link is through the Indians' and the Star People's mutual connection with nature, with mystical energy, and with universal forces. These two groups speak the same "language," therefore, Indian lifetimes are easily remembered and even tend to haunt the Star Person. Therefore both groups find communications with the UFO beings extremely easy and natural.

American Indians and Star People manage to communicate with space intelligences even in the humdrum hassle of today's world. But imagine how dynamic and vivid the contact was when the white man had not yet come to the North American continent. Then there was only the natural, mystical way. No one pointed a finger and laughed at the person who reported a conversation with an alien being. Instead, the Indian man or woman who underwent such an experience was asked to speak at the tribal meeting, to tell the wonderful story of the encounter, again and again as the years passed.

If the American Indian needed guidance he had only to turn to the sky gods and spirits for input and wisdom. He did not question where this knowledge came from nor did he dissect the experience. He simply valued it and learned from it. It was as natural as the stars that shone overhead. There is much that the human race can learn from the American Indian in his *oneness* with the Universe. There must develop an infinite respect for this wise cosmic citizen, and we must all do what we can to see that the Indian culture and way of life is not lost entirely.

If you are seeking true contact with the space brothers and sisters, we suggest you put down your book on advanced propulsion and take a walk out in nature, to a place where the American Indians have lived and worshipped. The power there will be indisputable, and an experience of cosmic nature is sure to await you!

8

AMERICAN INDIANS and THE STAR PEOPLE

One of the few white persons to walk among several of the Indian tribes of the South West is famed author Brad Steiger whose occult and metaphysical books have sold over 15 million copies worldwide. Tracing back their history for centuries, Brad has become convinced that the Amerindians have long had a tradition of contact with Star People and that these influences have become part of their traditions and life styles. In this chapter Brad explores many of the mystical legends of the Hopi in relationship to UFOs. His books *American Indian Magic* and *Mystical Legends of the Shamans* are available from *Inner Light Publications.*

Mrs. Eric Bluhm reported in the October 1972 issue of *Skylook*, a publication of the Mutual UFO Network, that she may have come across another case of UFO-related livestock mutilation while vacationing with her husband in the west. It was while they were on an all-day Jeep trek in Canyon de Chelly, Arizona that Mrs. Bluhm noticed a dead donkey with a peculiar strip, approximately nine inches wide, cut from its neck.

The flesh has been sliced away by a skillful butcher, and Mrs. Bluhm was at once reminded of the famous case of Snippy, the horse that had allegedly been carved and eviscerated by ufonauts.

During lunch break, she asked Johnny, the Navajo guide, if he had ever seen any UFOs. Johnny admitted that he sometimes saw silver round things flying overhead when he was in the canyons.

When Mrs. Bluhm pressed Johnny for an identification of the objects, "merely shrugged in typical Indian fashion." Later, though, Mrs. Bluhm stated in her report, she learned that Johnny's mother had reported sighting UFOs in the canyons on at least two occasions.

Although I, too, was at first presented with many a shrug "in typical Indian fashion" when I first began speaking to native American friends about UFOs, I have since come to know that nearly all of the tribes have a rich and varied tradition of an interaction with the "Sky People" or "Star People" that is as extensive as fairy lore is among the natives of the British Isles. Amerindians, for example, have been aware of "magic circles" left by the Star People just as their British counterparts know of the "fairy rings," and the modern UFO investigator examines the strange, scorched circles left in farmers' fields and meadows.

Interestingly, the guide lines for Amerindian-Star People interaction, which were no doubt evolved over centuries of trial and error, bear amazing similarities to the observations complied by British and European countryfolk regarding the fairies and the woodland gentry. And just as there are legends in Great Britain and Europe which suggest that in certain instances the melding between humankind and their other-worldly companions becomes extremely intimate, so are there Amerindians who believe that such a blending may have taken place between their own ancestors and those from the stars.

HOPI PROPHESIES TO BE FULFILLED

"I doubt very much if you will find another Indian who will tell you this,"said an Amerindian friend of mine (who must remain nameless since he has already received criticism from tribal elders for revealing too much about the Medicine Power to me), "but I don't believe there is any doubt whatsoever that there are Indian people on the face of this Earth who did not originate on this planet. I tend to think that once the Hopi prophecies are carried out and their revelations are made known, they will bear this out."

When non-Indian Paul Solem, a UFO contactee, told the media that he had been sent to the Hopi Reservation to "call down" UFOs to present the Hopis with a sign, he did manage to produce what the waiting, skeptical press called "a flying saucer." (It looked like a star—almost. It rose in the sky, stopped, hovered, wavered to one side and then continued across the sky, repeating the maneuvers," reported Joe Kraus, Managing Editor of the *Prescott Courier*, on August 9, 1970). But Solem also provoked yet another split among the traditional Hopi, some of whom believe in a tribal descendency from ufonauts and an ancient culture, while others favor the more orthodox anthropological description of their lineage. Chief Dan Katchongva, however, said that both the division and the UFOs are in fulfillment of the old prophecies foretelling the Great Purification:

"A petroglyph near Mishongnovi on Second mesa shows flying saucers and travel through space. The arrow on which the dome-shaped object rests, stands for travel through space. The Hopi maiden on the dome shape represents purity. Those Hopi who survive Purification Day will be taken to other planets. We, the faithful Hopi, have seen the ships and know they are true. We have watched nearly all our brethren lose faith in the original teachings and go off on their own course. Near Oraibi was closely shown the Plan of Life, and we are gathered here to await our True White Brother."

LOST TRIBES

Paul Solem claims that the UFOs are piloted by a people descended from the Ten Lost Tribes of Israel. The Hopi share this lineage, and the Great Star which led them to Oraibi was a guiding UFO. Certain Hopis state that the ships are manned by Kachinas, entities which are portrayed in traditional Hopi dances.

"Many people have said that our picture-craft is nothing but primitive doodling," White Bear, a Hopi historian and traditionalist remarked, "but centuries and centuries ago, the Hopi drew a jet airplane on a rock which depicted our people arriving from the birthplace of our fathers. Yes, centuries ago, we had a picture-craft of a flying saucer."

There are certain risks involved in ascribing "ancient astronaut" interpretations to petroglyphs (stone carvings) and pictographs (stone paintings) which may have been inspired by an artistic flight of fancy rather than an alien spaceship. "Domed space helmets" often turn out to be representations of horned headdresses, exaggerated in size to denote a chief's prowess and acumen or a medicine man's power and skill. But since the matter of petroglyph renderings offering a tangible record of Amerindian interaction with the Star People has been raised, I do believe there are some petroglyphs and pictographs that are worthy of examination from the ancient astronaut point of view.

Thirty miles northeast of Price, Utah, is the beginning of one of the most unusual canyons in the nation, Nine Mile Canyon. Prior to 1100 A.D., the Fremont culture occupied the canyon, and the records they left in the form of petroglyphs and pictographs comprise the heaviest concentration of rock art in the world today.

The Fremont people developed their own art style, which, interestingly, was typified by horned, trapezoidal-bodied, human-like "anthropomorphs." Were these creatures somehow symbolic of nature spirits? Or did they truly represent visitations by being decidedly different from the Fremont people's other Amerindian neighbors?

In one dramatic petroglyph in Nine Mile Canyon, one may view an unusual depiction of one of these horned (an ancient astronaut enthusiast might say, "antenna-sprouting"), anthropomorphic figures. In this instance, the creature is standing before a row of upraised human hands, which seem to imply awe, reverence, or fear. To the anthropomorph's left, there is a disc-like object. To the disc's left, there is an upside-down anthropomorph faintly etched in the stone.

Another petroglyph in Nine Mile Canyon shows what is definitely a scorpion in the middle of two mysterious figures. Some authorities have said that the etchings represent a fish and a tree, perhaps worked in an experimental style by some venturesome Fremont artist. Others, though, have wondered if the petroglyph might not give homage to a dramatic energy or power assigned to a strange-blob-like object that had the ability to "sting like a scorpion."

John Magor, writing in his excellent Canadian UFO Report, describes a most intriguing "flying object" pictograph which is located in a natural grotto near Christina Lake, B.C. The drawing depicts a white disc with black wing-like protuberances, hovering over four figures who appear to have bent their knees in an attitude of reverence. Squiggly lines, perhaps suggestive of rays of light, emanate from the top of the object. Longer, more irregular lines, extend from the bottom of the disc, possibly portraying smoke or fire.

"Although it was a practice of these primitive artists to depict exactly what they saw," Magor writes, "they must have been limited by their inability to draw in depth. Consequently, instead of illustrating the central object edgewise . . . the artist may have tilted it to show its discoid appearance while retaining the wind-like rim outline that surely would have impressed him."

FANTASTIC ROCK PAINTING

Despite the limitations of paint upon rock, Magor feels that the unknown artist showed great skill in conveying the idea of something extraordinary in the air.

"Because of its comparative size," Magor says, "it is obviously not a bird. And just as obviously because of its shape (perhaps that is why the artist retained the winged look) it is not the sun."

Magor feels that the touch of real brilliance on the part of the Amerindian artist lay in the use of four human figures. "Not only do they lend size and height to the object, but by their suggestion of a worshipful attitude, they create the impression that this was an event of rare spiritual importance. We can assume that the people they represent thought a god had come to visit, just as ancient scriptures—if we care to make the interpretation—describe visits elsewhere by gods in their chariots."

Perhaps, though, the pictograph is not all that old. Could the Amerindian artist have been depicting his tribes' reaction to the first terrestrial aircraft which paid them a low overflight visit?

Magor answers this question by seeking out reference volumes which date the pictographs in the area as prior to 1860. Quoting from John Corner's Pictographs in the Interior of British Columbia:

"The fact remains that the Indians of the Interior Salish (whose territory included Christina Lake) and Kootenay tribes and their ancestors were productive painters of pictographs from some unestablished date until about 1860, when suddenly, and still unaccountably, the artists put aside their paints and applicators to paint no more."

In the same issue of *Canadian UFO Report*, Magor included an article from the *New Westminster Columbian*, in which staff reporter Alan Jay drew some rather astonishing parallels between the illustrations of "gods" and "visiting chariots" in Erich von Daniken's books and the rock paintings of the early Canadian Indians.

To quote a sample from Jays research: "A drawing photographed by Von Daniken in the Sahara Desert shows a figure holding what appears to be a short rod totally enclosed in what the author claims is an early representation of a space sphere. The Mara Lake (British Columbia) drawing shows a crowned figure holding two strangely shaped objects in each hand. Their function is unknown, but they closely resemble the flanged ray guns so often seen in science-fiction comic strips. The figure is totally enclosed in a sphere identical to the one depicted in the Sahara Desert drawing."

In one of his asides to a reporter, John Magor rightly reminds his readers that such interpretations can prove to be very tricky. For example, Magor points out, similar spheres are seen around rock paintings where there is no hidden meaning. The early Amerindian artists had a habit of crowding pictures together on their painting surfaces. Enclosure of a pictograph may have been a means of avoiding confusion between the story of one painting and that of another.

LUNAR MODULE

More impressive similarities between Amerindian pictographs and "chariots of the gods" would seem to be the cone-shaped, rocket-like objects discovered near Cayuse Creek and Kootenay Lake. Quoting again from Alan Jay's article in the *Columbian:*

"Yet another rock painting at Cayuse Creek shows what is clearly a cone-shaped rocket with smoke and flame trailing behind it. And it contains a single humanoid figure apparently holding on to the inner wall of the rocket.

"A ... pictograph near Kootenay Lake depicts the same kind of enclosed vehicle, also containing a single humanoid figure. The drawing also shows sections resembling the firing stages of a modern lunar rocket and two appendages closely resembling the retractable landing legs of a lunar space module."

John Corner's book also reveals pictographs of egg-shaped objects from which wavy lines emanate. Magor does not feel, as some interpreters have suggested, that these rock paintings are depicting the sun shining on water. The pictographs remind him of contemporary UFO descriptions of glowing egg-shaped objects.

"The wavy lines underneath might have been the artist's way of showing the object was in motion," Magor theorizes. Or since early Amerindian craftsmen were meticulous about visual impression, the lines might indicate some kind of vapor trail.

In a Fraser Lake, B.C. pictograph, there are no rays protruding from the upper surface, which, in Magor's opinion, "virtually eliminates any notion that the artist was drawing the sun." Amerindian artists' more obvious symbol of the sun was a circle with short straight lines emanating from the entire circumference. In the Fraser Lake pictograph, however, only the zigzag lines underneath are shown, "suggesting once more the idea of motion or propulsion."

Wisely, John Magor continually cautions his readers about ascribing to strange petroglyphs and pictographs depictions of early interactions between Amerindians and entities from "out there." There is one other petroglyph, however, which may bear enough circumstantial evidence to merit additional investigation—or at least theorization.

At Roberson Point, Prince Rupert, B.C., there is an unusual intaglio (incised carving) of the outline of a human-like figure. In Tsimshian legend the petroglyph is known as the "man who fell from heaven."

John Magor comments, "Perhaps we can accept this as a literal definition. The carving is so utterly unlike anything else of early Indian origin on the West Coast that its history must be extraordinary.

"One idea is that the Tsimshians living there discovered the body of an exceptionally strange man in their camp, and with some logic, decided that he must have dropped from the sky. Perhaps they conceived this carving as an open grave to allow the stranger's spirit to return home. If it is a grave, it was certainly not intended for any of the Indians' own kind. Among northern native groups the tendency is to shelter graves, not expose them . . . ."

It would not have been at all remarkable for the early Amerindians of any tribe to believe that a stranger might have fallen to Earth from the sky. Amerindians adhered to that universal belief which holds that the stars are the residences of spiritual beings who have a definite connection with, and a mysterious relation to, human souls.

A recognition of the symbolic relationship between the Star People and Homo sapiens was prevalent in the early Egypt of Ramses the Great. The Persians kissed their hands at the stars in reverence and pictured them governed by presiding spirits. The Chinese believed that the stars were the abode of gods who influenced the actions of Mankind. Some scholars have suggested that the ancient art of astrology began because of the universal belief among early Man that dwellers of the stars participated in the destiny of each man and woman on Earth.

FIRST STAR CHILD?

The following tradition, related by one of the Iowa tribes, is but an echo of similar accounts which could be told by many other Amerindian people:

Many years ago, a young child observed a star that attracted him more than any other. As the child grew to manhood, his attachment increased.

One day while hunting, he sat down, travel-worn, weary with his lack of success. At that time his beloved star appeared to him, comforted him with encouraging words, then conducted him to a place where he found a great variety of game. From this time on the young man showed a wonderful improvement in the art of hunting, and soon became celebrated in this pursuit.

During the vision quest, if properly performed with requisite humility and courage, each supplicant would receive his guide. As one who had been initiated into the Winnebago tradition recalled for me:

"I spent 12 days fasting, awaiting my guide. I had many creatures, including a beautiful deer, come up to me and allow me to pet them. The deer, especially, wanted to stay. But I had been told that if I did not want to accept a form of life that offered itself to me, I should thank it for coming, tell it of its beauty, its strength, its intelligence, but tell it also that I was seeking one greater.

"On the twelfth day, an illuminated form appeared before me. Although it seemed composed primarily of light, it did have features and was clothed in a long robe. 'You I have waited for,' I said.

It replied, 'You have sought me and you I have sought.' Then it faded away.

"On the evening that each boy was required to appear before the council to tell of his experience, my guide was accepted

Brad Steiger meditates outside sacred Indian ground in Sedona, Arizona.

as genuine. I don't think any young boy could have fooled that tribal council. They knew when the boy had had a real experience and when he had used something as an excuse to get back to the reservation and get something to eat.

"One thing we were taught is that we must never call upon our guides until we have exhausted every bit of physical energy and mental resource possible. After we have employed every last ounce of our own reserve, we might call upon our guide and it would appear."

In addition to guidance, several Amerindian legends suggest a more physical kind of interaction between the Star People and the native population.

The Chippewa tell of a star that was driven out of its home in the sky because of a quarrel which had developed among the Star People. The star would wander from tribe to tribe, and it was often seen hovering over the campfires when the people were preparing for sleep. Although most men and women were quite fearful of the Star, one Chippewa maiden came to admire and love it.

In midsummer, the young girl, on going into the woods to pick berries, found herself caught in a sudden storm which lifted her into the star. That was when her tribesmen knew that the star had also come to love their beautiful child.

THE SAGA OF WHITE HAWK

Another Chippewa tale could easily be transposed to the British Isles and the fairy tradition.

A young hunter named White Hawk was crossing a prairie when he discovered a peculiar circle on the ground. The circle appeared to have been formed by a beaten footpath, and the curious hunter decided to conceal himself in the tall grass nearby and learn what had formed the mysteriously trodden area.

After White Horse had lain in vain for a time, he heard the sound of distant music coming from the air. His eyes were drawn to a cloud that was descending from afar. As it drew nearer, the hunter saw that it was not a cloud at all, but a basket device in which he saw 12 beautiful maidens, each gracefully striking a drum. Soon the basket touched the ground, the young maidens leaped out and began to dance.

The young hunter was entranced by their beauty and the grace of their dance. The drumming sound now seemed to be coming from the basket, and each of the young maidens struck a shining ball at each step as they moved lightly around the circle. In his delight, White Hawk reached out to touch the dancer nearest him. But the moment the maidens saw him, they jumped back into the basket and were instantly withdrawn into the heavens.

The saddened hunter returned to his lodge, bewailing his misfortune. At night his slumbers were haunted by the sounds of the celestial music and the vision of the lovely Star Maidens. He resolved to return to the magic circle and wait until the maidens returned.

Disguising himself with the hides of opossums, White Hawk's vigil at the circle was at last rewarded by the sight of the lowering basket and the delightful strains of the sweet music. Once the Star Maidens were engaged in their dance, White Hawk began stalking the girl nearest him. But again, the Star Maidens saw him and sprang for the safety of their basket.

One who appeared to be their leader said, "Perhaps he has come to show us how the game is played by earthly beings." But the other maidens shouted for ascent into the sky.

On his third attempt, White Hawk disguised himself as a stump near the magic circle, and he successfully captured one of the Star Maidens. With gentle actions and kind words, he brought her to his lodge and made her his bride.

Although the passing months produced a lovely boy child from their union, the Star Wife grew weary with the tribal confines. She longed to return to the stars. When White Hawk was away on a hunt, the Star Wife ventured to the magic circle and summoned a basket to take her to Star Land.

White Hawk was disconsolate with grief and spent many seasons sorrowing for his lost wife and son. The Star Chief, at the same time, was observing his grandchild's longing for his earthly father. In a gesture of compassion and wisdom, the Star Chief commanded the Star Wife to offer White Hawk a visit to Star Land in return for "a specimen of each kind of bird and animal that he kills in the chase." White Hawk gratefully accepted the Star Chief's offer, and the legend ends with the Star Wife consenting to resume life among her husband's people.

The Amerindians divided their supernatural visitors and companions into two categories, those glowing lights in the sky, (the Star People) and those who inhabited field and forest, the *Puckwudjinies*.

THE VANISHING PEOPLE

Here we have one of those intricate cross-cultural references which prove to be so intriguing. *Puckwudjinies* is an Algonquin name which signifies "little vanishing people." *Puck* is a generic of the Algonquin dialect, and its exact similarity to the "Puck" of the British fairy tradition is remarkable. Puck, or Robin Goodfellow, is the very personification of the woodland elf; he is Shakespeare's merry wanderer in *Midsummer's Night Dream,* "sweet Puck," who declares what fools we mortals be.

Puck is no doubt derived from the old Gothic *puke*, a generic name for minor spirits in all the Teutonic and Scandinavian dialects. *Puke* is cognate with the German *spuk*, a goblin, and the Dutch *spook*, a ghost. Then there is the Irish *pooka* and the Cornish "pixie." To break down *Puckwudjini* even further and concentrate on its suffix, we find *jini*, the Arab's *jini* or genie, the magical imp.

The Amerindians' two categories for the phenomenon reminds me of John A. Keel's statement in his recent book, *The Mothman Prophecies*: "The UFO phenomenon . . . can be divided into two main parts. The first and most important part consists of the mysterious aerial lights which appear to have an intelligence of their own . . . The second part . . . consists of the cover or camouflage for the first part, the 'meandering nocturnal lights' as the Air Force has labeled them . . . Explanatory manifestations have accompanied them always, and these manifestations have always been adjusted to the psychology and beliefs of each particular period in time. . ."

The fairy lover is a recognized type and figure in folklore, and there are countless references made of amorous relations between the fairy folk and humans of both sexes. In like manner, the legends of the Amerindians contain many accounts of Star Wives and Husbands. Although there may be individual cultural differences from tribe to tribe, the basic accounts of the Star Husband could be outlined in the following way:

A young girl sleeping outside the lodge or wigwam is taken away during the night by the Star People. She awakens to find herself in a different world and the bride of a Star Husband. Although life is pleasant in Star Land, the girl grows lonesome for her own people. From time to time, she is permitted to look into a hole through which she can see her tribesmen. But if she grows too despondent, she is permitted to return to her tribe, usually after performing a task which seems to her to be nonsensical. If a child has been produced by their union, it is usually required that she leave her offspring with her Star Husband and his people.

In the fairy tradition, there are numerous accounts in which men and women were kidnapped by the fairies never again to return to their own villages. In the Amerindian legends, men and women seem almost always to be returning to their own kind after producing offspring, performing a required task, or presenting a gift of Earth products. In most of the legends of the Amerindians and the Star People, nothing is forced, and there are few accounts of violence between them. The only exceptions would seem to arise in instances wherein an Amerindian trespasses in an area which is considered sacred to the Star People.7

STRANGE DEATH

An account of a mysterious, possibly UFO-related, disappearance with a suggestion of violence toward an Amerindian appeared, of all places, in the July 1967 issue of *Sports Afield*. According to Russell Annabel's article, "Smart Injun Trick or UFO?," the Denna Indians of Alaska are well aware of the Sky People and even decorate their totem symbols and spirit houses with their sign: a horizontal slash, the outline of a hump on top of it.

Annabel tells of an Indian friend of his who found the two-year-old wreckage of an aircraft that had gone down after managing to send a final message which had been heard on the cabin radio of a trapper.

"Mayday . . . Mayday," the pilot had called, "over the Talkeetnas . . . brilliant green light all around us . . . both engines have cut . . . the thing . . ."

Then, two years later, while tracking a bear, the Indian located the wreckage with its frozen corpses. One man had not died right away. He had managed to draw a picture on the side of the plane—a picture of a flying saucer, or, to the eyes of the Indian, the sign of the Sky People.

It was Denna tradition that the Sky People had landed frequently on Denna Mountain in the past and still patrolled the area and occasionally made off with someone. No "medicine" was powerful enough to work against the Sky People.

Annabel's Indian friend may have proved that point with the ultimate in visual demonstrations. Having got himself in minor trouble with the law through a misunderstanding, the Indian fled into the mountains. Annabel and a brother-in-law of the fugitive set out to bring him back to straighten out the matter.

The Indian had left a clear trail in the snow, then suddenly, the snowshoe tracks abruptly ended in a bleak opening on a footslope of a mountain. The man's brother-in-law studied the tracks carefully, then issued his pronouncement:

"Wasilla went up . . . something took him. He didn't have any warning. He didn't see it or hear it, because he didn't stop to look up. He didn't have time to fight. Something just grabbed him and snatched up into the sky."

The incident occurred 20 years ago, Annabel tells us, and neither Wasilla nor his remains have ever been found.

Whatever the truth may be in the account which Russell Annabel reported, the majority of Amerindian Medicine People today believe that the Star People and Spirit Guardians of the Earth Mother are becoming active at this time in an effort to aid Mankind to survive the coming Great Purification of the planet.

AN IMPORTANT VISION

On Aug. 2, 1974, during a lovely and meaningful ceremony, I was adopted into the Wolf Clan of the Seneca tribe by the Repositor of Seneca Wisdom, Twylah Nitsch. At a private ceremony, I was also initiated into the Wolf Clan Medicine Lodge. My adoptive name is *Hat-yas-swas* (He Testifies), and I was charged with continuing to seek out and share universal truths.

In October 1974, Twylah received a vision about the role of the Medicine People in the coming days of strife, chaos, and cleansing.

"We are presently here because we are aware of the coming cleansing of Mother Earth," Twylah said. "Man has exerted an imbalance on her way of life; he has exhausted her natural resources. Medicine People must retain and guard the use of her gifts, or she will no longer be able to nurture her creatures. After the Earth Mother has been cleansed, Medicine People must seed the decrees of the Creator in the next world.

"When the transition occurs, our spiritual light will guide and protect us as we evolve as people of wisdom and as messengers of the decrees of the Creator. Each messenger, according to the level his gifts and abilities have developed, will assist others in seeking the Pathway of Peace."

Will there be assistance from other entities and intelligences from other dimensions of existence?

"Yes," Twylah answered. "All over this world and on other worlds there are Messengers sitting in council. They will come to convene with us. This has happened before, and this communication will continue for time eternal."

If the Medicine predictions are correct, we may soon be observing the Star People ourselves.

SECRETS OF THE TOTEM

There are few researchers whose work has reached the depth and scope of L. Taylor Hansen. A frequent contributor over the years for such astute publications as *Fate* and *Search*, the author of *Secrets of the Totem* literally lived among the Amerindian tribes. His work *He Walked the Americas* (Amherst Press) delves into the historical legends that Christ—during the years of his life that could not be traced—actually ended up in North America—and taught the tribes much in the way of spiritual values. Though this chapter does not reflect this research, it is an interesting look into the Totem beliefs held by nearly all the tribes of this country.

The totem of the turtle is a significant bit of symbolism in the ancient history of man. Here we learn some of its history and its secret meanings.

It was during one of the Pueblo festivals that I first saw the Dance of the Turtle. It was not the worn and picturesquely irregular housetops of the Ancient Zuni nor the colorful crowd, but the dancers' costumes which held my eyes.

The men had top-knots of macaw feathers, with three eagle plumes hanging down the back. (Strange, is it not, that macaw feathers should form part of a ceremonial costume in the desert?)

Both the men and women of the dance were dressed in white. The men wore white girdles, the women flowing white mantles. They flashed with silver and turquoise, and in that hot desert sun my thoughts fled back to the Mayas.

I was remembering again Uxmal under its thick covering of jungle. I was particularly remembering the House of the Turtle. (so-called because of its sculptured motif) and its simple and elegant line of round columns encircling the beautiful edifice and catching the early, slanting rays of the morning sun.

I was also remembering that Bancroft spoke of a pavement of slate tiles laid in copper in the vicinity of many turtle vases near the mouth of the river San Juan, while in Cinaca-Mecallo, where the remains or ruins cover an oval area similar to the shell of a turtle, "the material used in all the structures is a slate-like stone in thin blocks, joined by a cement which resembles in color and consistency, molten lead."

Perhaps this was but the earlier building material of the Itzaes, who later built largely with hewn limestone blocks laid in a cement which is much stronger than our average mortar. We know that the Itzaes were of The Turtle, because one plaque in Chichen Itza shows the figure of Itzamna, their national god, emerging from the shell of a turtle. Furthermore, the symbols and figures of the turtle and snake are almost inexplicably mingled in all the Mayan ruined cities, until we remember that in the oldest traditions—the Itzaes conquered the Chanes, or the people of the Snake, who were the first owners of the land, and who were "all descendants of the Great-Water-Serpent who crawled out of the sunrise sea."

Whence came these Itzaes? The trail seems to lead south. Not only the oldest turtle monuments are to be found in the zone of the Isthmus, but the glorious quetzal plumes which hung down from the top-knot of the Itzae head-dress pointed to a southern origin for their wearers, since the magnificent quetzal bird, possibly specially bred for untold ages before the breakup of the great aviaries of the ancients set it free, is a bird of the tropics. And it has ever been, along with the eagle and the macaw, the supreme bird of American royalty.

So in the pueblo Dance of the Turtle, I saw the wandering Itzaes, driven from their southern lands, trooping through the pueblo country, beautiful in their flowing white garments and resplendent in their waving quetzal plumes and their jewelry.

As is the way with Amerind lore, it was to be after a lapse of several years that I got my next clue to the wandering Itzae. It came from my Chippewa friend, Marksman (the Chippewa tribe speaks an Algonquian tongue). He had just returned to the shore of Keeweenaw Bay, Lake Superior, from a visit to one of the reservations of Minnesota where the Chippewas are lodged very close to their old enemies, the Sioux. (Incidentally the word Sioux is a disrespectful term given these people by their enemies and which in the typical grim humor of the Amerind, the tribe will not bother to deny or explain to the whites. The tribes' own name for themselves is The Dacotah.)

Marksman was busy describing a funny incident, when I interrupted him. He never did get to finish.

"Excuse me, Marksman, but I understood you to say that because the Chippewa had defeated the Sioux at your last tribal battle, the Chippewa had carved a big turtle upside-down?"

He nodded.

"Then the Turtle is the totem of the Sioux?"

He caught the excitement in my voice and nodded quietly. (To lift the mystery of the past even a little, he was willing to go to any length if it might prove that an enemy tribe once had a great past.)

"Tell me all you know of their pottery, it is a polished black ware?"

"Yes, black is their sacred color. Their god Wakon is supposed to dwell in The Black Hills."

"Do they have signs of the Venus Calendar? I mean, is the evening star important to them?"

"They say that they were organized by the evening star. And the chief village always has the name of the Evening Star."

"Do they worship volcanoes, and build pyramids?"

"Dunno about that. Their wigwams, they call 'em teepees, looks like mountains—white mountains smoking."

"You are right" I gasped, "And furthermore, the Aztec name for white peak is almost identical! Probably that is also why the Ciouan, Caddoan and Iroquoian tribes burned their captives. It was merely a ritualistic sacrifice to their Fire-god?"

"Sure. They burn Chippewa too."

In my mind many telescopic pictures flashed, which were of themselves only loose ends. The polished black pottery of the Mayas, so recently revived by the Pueblo. The most magnificent ruin of Mayan antiquity—the stupendous Temple of the Warrior, sometimes called the Temple of the Thousand Columns, and its repeated turtle-motif! The drooping feathered head-dress of the Dacotahs, which seemed to be a cross between that of the Mayas and that of the Aztecs! The polished black pottery of the Aztecs, particularly reserved for the elegant table of Montezuma.

Also there was that name Wakon. Its trail, too, led south, though it was more prepared for the dragon worship carrying an Amen name.

"Tell me, Marksman, what does this god Wakon look like?" It he a big snake, or a turtle?"

"No. Him all-e-same Thunderbird."

For a moment this stopped the trend of my speculations. I began to check over the name. Wakon was the great deity of the South Seas. He had sometimes been spoken of as coming in a fleet of ships. Dr. Buck in his *Vikings of the Sunrise*, said that this figure was probably of a real individual, and according to the old chant, checked to about the time of Christ or lst century A.D. Wakoyama is a coast town of Japan, yama meaning "mountain," and, incidentally, very close to the Zamma name for the old volcanic fire-god.

We next hear of Wako in the Americas where a town near the Peruvian coast is named for him. From there we have the clear legends of Matto Grosso, The Waikanoes and Tukanoes tell of their great god Wako who came up the Amazon in a fleet of ships. He was a bearded white man who performed many miracles of healing, taught them many arts and, after staying a year, sailed away. The Waikanoes trace their descent, incidentally, to a water-snake or great water-monster, while the ruling Tukanoes have the totem of a great bird. The fact that their neighbors have a black polished pottery may be but a coincidence. Both tribes in physical type and in domestic plants suggest a south-sea-island background.

However, the long-headed, hawk-nosed, red-skinned, fire-worshipping Karibs who poured in from the Antilles in their long war-canoes and spread both up and down the Atlantic coast, driving the round-headed Waikano and Tukano tribes far into Matto Cross, also revere the name Wako. The Kiribi had a leader named Wakna who is similar to the Great Wako. He too, dressed in flowing white garments, came in a fleet of ships and performed great miracles of healing. Their neighbor and brother-tribe, the Summo, say that they were sired by Masya-kana and their mother was Itiuana. The first name is not recognizable but the latter is the Itzae Itamma in another dialect.

The Totem and Kachina played an important part in the Indian rituals.

If we were to base the connection between the Dacotah of North America and the fierce Karib on only the likeness of fireworship and black pottery, it would indeed be too thin to pass the law of averages. However, when we realize that both tribes also built palisaded villages, had a definite trace of an ancient and fast-disintegrating caste system as well as the ancient Venus calendar, used women-slaves, as well as sometimes allowing their own women to become warriors, and told time by notched sticks, quippus, and seeds enclosed in a gourd, we are pressing the law of averages. Nor have we in any way exhausted the list, but rather let us say we have only scratched the surface, leaving this tremendous joy of research to a later and more careful student.

It is a curious fact that these culture-trails of the Antilles, which are so strong in the Muskhogeans, and particularly in the Natchez, play out in the Dacotahs and the Iroquois to mere suggestions, showing the much greater distance in time the latter tribes are from the common center. However, we must remember that the Dacotahs, whose holding of women-slaves denigrated the place of their own women, still allowed the old women a hand in the choosing of a new chief, and John Carver, a traveller in the eighteenth century, found them telling the passage of time by the aid of the notched stick and the quippu—a realm which we particularly link to the Inca!

Nor would this be all that a later student in comparative research will discover. He will find a tremendous likeness of ceremony. This would not be confined

to the striking similarities of the rituals of "Lighting the New Fire," or "Renewing the Sacred Fire," but would extend to other ceremonies. But that is with the future. That same student will also discover many "steading the fire" myths of the North American tribes which throw interesting sidelights upon his problem. For these myths do not pertain to fire as such, which man has had since he could walk upright, but to this ritualistic Eternal-Fire which seems to have entered America from the Antilles.

Perhaps the most interesting fact about these old fire-worshippers is the manner in which they differ. Most of the North American tribes expose their dead, as to the Algonkquin Eagle Totem. But the true Karibs seat them on a stone bench, in a stone-lined circular or oval grave, in such a manner that they will be facing the rising sun. Similar graves to this are to be found on the coast of California, near the vicinity of Santa Barbara and in Florida, on an old land surface which runs out into the sea. (Later Karib tribes buried their dead under their long-canoes or cremated them in the Sacred-Fire.) It should be also noticed that they faced the great golden disc whose intricately sculptured face was melted down by the Spanish.

There is one more curious connection to the Turtle. In old China, where the Turtle and the Snake were considered to be black and hold the northern color-direction of their old zodiac, they are thought to have had dominion over water, which is said to be the black element. Furthermore, according to their mythology, their written language comes from the mystic markings upon the shell of the

Turtle, and thus they are indebted to the totem for their script. China shows signs of early attempts to thrust the Turtle into the class of evil or "untouchable" gods but in Japan the turtle is much revered.

What is the ancient tie which binds the elegant Itazaes, the architects who fashioned the Temple of the Warriors, the savage Karibs, and the yelling followers of Crazy Horse who wiped out the forces of General Custer? From what volcano, possibly now lost beneath the blue-green waves of the Atlantic, did these immigrants, or possibly refugees from a geological catastrophe, bring their Sacred-fire? Perhaps, at least in our generation, one asks the question as vainly as he might if he personally addressed one of these old mummies seated upon his stone bench, staring out to sea. Who can say with our present knowledge what land of memory his sightless eyes may be seeking?

References:

Joyce: *Central American Archaeology.*
Bancroft: *Native Races,* Vol. IV, Antiquities.
Hewett: *Ancient Life in Mexico and Central America.*
Clements R. Markham: Incas of Peru.
Buck: Vikings of the Sunrise (The book *Temple of the Warriors* contains some excellent views of this edifice for the illustrator)
A. L. Kroeber: *Native Culture of the Southwest.* University of Calif. Press (Amer.Arch. and Eth. Series.)
G. D. Gower: *Northern and Southern Affiliation of Antillean Culture in America* Anthrop. Assn. No. 35, 1927
A Sketch of Chinese Arts and Crafts by H. A. Strong of the Peking Chinese Booksellers, Inc. 1926.

PLAYGROUND OF THE GODS

Is it merely coincidence that a good number of sightings have taken place above sacred Indian spiritual places or over the resesrvations of the various tribes? Or is it just more proof that the Sky Gods are keeping a watchful eye on their friends? This reports filed by John Mangor which originally appeared as a copyrighted story in the *Canadian UFO Report* typifies many such strange occurrences over the sacred ground. From the details of this chapter it is apparent that the UFO phenomena is an ongoing occurrence above the Playground of the Gods.

One of the most spectacular natural features of North America is a gigantic gash, 50 miles wide in places, running from the northern wilds of British Columbia down into Montana. It is the Rocky Mountain Trench, source of the great Columbia River that escapes northward from the valley before turning right around to find its Pacific outlet far to the South in Oregon.

Hemmed on each side by mountain ranges, the Trench was the basin of an inland sea half a billion years ago, and today its rock walls are encrusted with the relics of marine life strikingly out of context with this towering countryside so distant from the sea.

A landscape of magnificent contrast from its fertile bed to its snow-brushed peaks, the Trench looks like a playground of the gods. And perhaps it truly is, for

here there is a seemingly endless record of visits from the sky.

Perhaps the best introduction to the UFO story of the Trench lies in the lifelong experiences of Mrs. Dino DeHart who grew up in the valley and has an intimate acquaintance with the tales of the Indians who were there uncounted years before David Thompson, first white man to explore the Columbia.

As a little girl of nine, which in her words was "a long time ago," she had her first hint that this was a land of strange happenings. She was with her mother, an Indian woman of strong religious leaning, in a buggy drawn by a pair of horses plodding carefully through the night along a narrow dirt road. On the other side of the river was their house, invisible in the darkness.

Suddenly, the whole valley was bathed in a soft white light. They could see their house as clearly as in daytime, as well as the river, their neighbors' houses, and the hills beyond. Excitedly the girl tugged her mother's arm, begging her to look. But her mother's hands were clasped in prayer and her eyes were closed. Surely, to her, this was a visitation.

In later years, Mrs. DeHart told us, she heard many Indian stories (she and her husband live close to an Indian reserve) of strange lights and sights in the valley. One that particularly impressed her was the tale of a great "wagon" appearing in the sky. It had large "wheels" and moved so smoothly it seemed to be floating on water. Mrs. DeHart herself saw another eerie occurrence when a hill about half a mile from her place suddenly lit up one night as if bathed in a floodlight. The illumination was so strong she and all the others there could see in detail the small sharp peak of the hill. In those same years her sister and brother-in-law had the bewildering experience one night of seeing their house glowing in a weird light as they climbed uphill toward it. In each case the lights went out as abruptly and inexplicably as they had appeared.

Mrs. DeHart's family was again brought in personal touch with these mystifying incidents when her son, with several companions, saw a light dash up a mountainside with the speed of an express train. In fact, for size and brightness, it might well have been a locomotive headlight, but there was no vehicle on earth that could have scaled those heights in such a manner.

Mrs. DeHart has heard of other incidents from her friends, but the one that remains most vivid in her mind is one she witnessed herself. It happened in the beginning of June, 1954.

"I was in the kitchen working on a new recipe and not having much luck with it," she said. "So I decided to give up and go to bed as it was about one o'clock in the morning.

"I had just turned the lights out when the whole room was lit up by a pink light coming through the window. There's nothing near our place that would make such a light, and I couldn't imagine what it would be, so I opened the window and looked out.

"Right outside there was this strange thing going by in the air. It looked metallic, like highly polished aluminum, and it was shaped like a big hat. Around the part where the band would be, just above the brim, there were three oval-shaped windows, or whatever they really were, and that is where the light was coming from. They were as bright as car headlights, and each light had two colors. Around the outside was a greenish color, and inside this, filling most of the light, was the pink color that was coming through the windows. The colors reminded me of the inside of an abalone shell." (Though somewhat stronger in hue than mother-of-pearl)."

While Mrs. DeHart was able to note general details of the craft, including shadowy lines on the surface that gave her the impression they were seams between metal plates, it was the light of the windows that held her attention. In her few seconds of sighting before the southbound craft moved out of view on her left—suggesting a speed of 50 m.p.h. or so—she noticed it traveled with an undulating motion and the lights changed with the same rhythm. As the object floated up the lights brightened, and as it came down they dimmed.

The witness remembers being able to stare at the light without being bothered by the glare. (Later with her husband's help, after explaining where she saw it, she figured it was about 100 feet up and 400 feet away). And she remembers one other thing which blends enchantingly into this story of almost Oriental magic.

"I sometimes think my ears must have been playing tricks," she said, "yet I feel sure it really did happen. Each time the thing climbed to the top of its wavy flight, I thought I heard a faint sound coming from it. It sounded like Chinese chimes."

* * *

In case the impression is formed that strange lights in the Trench are simply some sort of Indian legend, let's consider next an extraordinary scene observed by a young married school-teacher.

Although as far as we know she was the sole witness, one only has to listen to her deeply considered and articulate account of the incident to appreciate she went through an experience just as vivid and unexplainable as she described it.

At the time of the incident the witness, who prefers her name be withheld, was driving on the valley highway south of the town of Invermere on her way to a friend's house for a game of bridge. It was an evening in November, 1969. She remembers the time well because it was the start of the bridge season, and she is fond of the game. This point is important as it means she felt particularly keen and free of tiredness in anticipating the evening ahead.

Her route was along a stretch of highway with which she was completely familiar. It took her through an undeveloped section of land which in the darkness, might have been difficult to identify had she not known the road so well. Ahead on the left she could see the lights of the local bowling-alley.

"On my right was a section where there are never any lights at all," she said. "It's a large depression formed by a dried-up creek bed and an old abandoned road. I had never seen a light there before, but that night there was one.

"It was a green luminescence—a pool of controlled light. It was the sort of glow you see over a lighted swimming pool at night. If it had been a camper's light or something like that, I'm sure I would have recognized it. This light was strange."

It was so strange, in fact, the witness felt that somehow the light was not limited to the area she was observing. She had the impression that momentarily her car was lit up, as if a piece had broken off to trace her for a second or two.

The witness found this a difficult point to explain and we do not pretend to have grasped it. But, without putting words in her mouth, we suggest a bush or forest fire might offer comparison. Often these are spread by an unseen agency when a section ignites that is far beyond the reach of any spark. Obviously no fire was involved in this particular case, but evidently the effect of the light, like heat from a fire, spread invisibly from its central source.

The light was strange in another way—it turned her car radio off.

Jim Statham

Mrs. Janice Schneider (left), Mrs. Lorraine Goodwin & sons.

Radium Hot Springs Pool

Mountain behind Hot Springs pool.

"Anyway, that's how it seemed," she said. "It stopped playing about the same time I first saw the light and it started again just after I had passed."

Still another odd point was that the light made the witness herself feel strange, and this was due to something more than just seeing a light where no light should be.

"The whole thing happened exactly as I have said. I wasn't dreaming. I was surprised to see a light there but I know it was real. Yet somehow I felt emotionally involved and I wondered if maybe it all had something to do with me personally."

This part of her experience made what will probably be a lasting impact on the witness. Speaking about it to us two years later, she was obviously still deeply involved with it.

Like others involved in UFO experiences with emotional association, this witness had hesitated to discuss it with anyone but those closest to her.

"At first I thought someone might be trying to play tricks," she said of our first inquiry by phone. "But when I found out this wasn't so, I spoke to my husband about it and we both felt I should tell you exactly what happened."

We have no way of knowing how this incident fits into the total UFO puzzle. We are sure, however, that in putting what was a very personal experience on record, this witness has made a contribution that will help us that much farther toward a solution.

* * *

If a light did in fact track the school-teacher's car for a moment, her experi-

ence was fairly peaceful compared to those of some others who have been exposed to incidents on the Trench highway.

In October, 1969, (note this was just a month before the previous case) two sisters of Edgewater, B.C., Mrs. Lorraine Goodwin and Mrs. Janice Schneider, had the terrifying experience of having a UFO repeatedly dive at them while they were driving with their five children in the car.

The object, a brilliant light alternating between red and green, took up the attack soon after they had left Cranbrook, close to the international border, in the late afternoon to proceed north toward home. Zooming in from one side, the light almost landed on the car and stayed there momentarily before darting off to the side again. This performance was repeated several times over a distance of about 15 miles. The group became so alarmed that they nearly went in the ditch.

* * *

Alone in her car one winter night in 1969, Joanne Hammond, then 16, of Radium, was on her way to visit friends and had an encounter with a UFO so frightening that she has never since driven by herself at night.

"It came flying right toward the windshield until it was just two or three feet away, then it shot up and disappeared for a second," she recalled. "The next thing I know it came shooting at me from the driver's side before it again went over the car, just missing the window."

Completely shaken, Joanne started to speed up only to have the object take up pursuit.

"It had a golden light coming from it," she said, "and I knew it was following me because the light was shining in the rearview mirror. It lit up the whole inside of the car. I was doing about 70 miles an hour by then and still it came after me."

After a mile or two the object gave up the chase when they came to a point where a few people were walking beside the road. When she later met her friends they immediately saw something was wrong and soon learned what had happened.

Despite her fright, Joanne formed a clear impression of the object's appearance.

"When it first came toward me, it looked round in front with a hump on top. But when it shot up over the car it looked more triangular. It had two wings that tapered off and right behind in the middle was a narrow tail about six inches long. The wings spread right across the windshield so I guess the whole thing was three or four feet wide altogether. It was very solid-looking, like metal, with the light coming out from the center of it."

During our interview, Joanne made a sketch of what she saw. Her drawing looked exactly like that of a miniature delta-wing aircraft. Then several weeks later, we were struck by this item from the *News* of Canberra, Australia, July 30, 1971. Headed FOUR DELTA UFO SEEN OVER LAKE, it said: "Two Canberra women who claim to have seen four unidentified flying objects over Lake George described them as dull-white delta-shaped objects."

There are two significant points here. One is that the delta-shaped craft seem to be showing up as an integral part of our visitor's equipment. The other is that Joanne's description was just as detailed as the Australian women's, though she was in a much more frightening position. The moral seems to be that UFO testimony should not be ignored just because the witness was excited and alone.

Among the friends who saw Joanne after the incident was Kern Clement of Windermere, foreman of a large Christmas-tree cutting operation. He still remembers how pale and upset she looked, but had no way of guessing that just a few nights later he would experience a UFO shock himself.

The incident occurred on a comparatively new mountain section of the Trans-Canada Highway called Roger's Pass. Though not part of the Trench, it is a split-second from it as the UFO flies.

Accompanied by a young woman from Windermere, Trudy Rexford, Clement was homeward bound in his truck when he noticed an unusual cloudy form against the sky ahead.

"It was like a cloud with a spotlight shining into it," he explained. "It looked very strange up there, not just because of the light but because it was a bright starry night and there wasn't another cloud in the sky."

Curious, he stopped the truck and the pair climbed out to have a better look. It was an invitation to action.

"As soon as we got out, that thing, whatever it was, started to come down right towards us." Clement said. "I told my friend to get in the truck and we both jumped back in."

However, when the object showed no sign of coming closer, they left the truck again to watch the performance.

"It was close enough to throw a little light on the highway," Clement said. "The light was circular and very white. I'd say it was about 10 feet in diameter. After a few seconds it took off again. It was gone in a flash."

He wryly added one more comment which probably would hold true for almost anyone else in the same spot.

"I have heard of other people seeing UFOs and always thought I would like to see one myself, close up. But when that happened, I was the first one back in that truck."

In approximately the same period Jim Statham, who is in charge of large Christmas-tree operations at Radium Hot Springs, noticed a strange flying object cross the valley from east to west. He was in his garden at about 8:00 p.m., and had a clear view of the whole incident.

"It was moving fast," he said. "In the time I saw it, about one minute, it came over the mountains from the east and disappeared well toward the mountains to the west.

"A rough estimate would place the distance at about 20 miles. But the object was no jet, or meteor.

"At the bottom it was darkish and looked round, and on top was this very bright light. It looked like a big star at first, but as it came closer I could see it had a definite shape. It made no noise. My son Tommy was with me and saw it, too."

Although there are continual signs of UFO activity over the Trench, it would be misleading to suggest that anyone can go there anytime and see something. Take the case of Bud Amy.

Amy is a well-known figure in the area. While he operates a popular amuse-ment park for youngsters a few miles south of Radium, he is perhaps better recognized for his handicraft work. His ornamental carvings have a wide market under the name of Amy Artcraft Products.

Being a man of imagination, Amy was quickly interested when UFOs began to draw public attention several years ago and made use of his time outdoors to keep watch. But though the time and place were fine, the results were not.

"I kept watching for 10 years without seeing a thing," he said. "Often I would get my sleeping bag and sleep outside on the lawn, but still no luck,"

All that changed on an August night in 1969—and it changed so dramatically it was almost as if he and his family were singled out for a personal visit.

"I was down by the highway, about 50 yards from the house, when it happened," he told us. "Suddenly I saw this thing with three soft glowing lights underneath coming in from the west. It was about three-quarters of the way on this side of the valley when I saw it, and it kept on coming until it passed right over the house! It was so close I could have hit it with a slingshot!"

Obviously it was not a kind of aircraft he had ever seen before. As it moved silently overhead he could see that the lights, positioned in triangular form, were set into the bottom of an object of circular shape, the light reflected outward enough to show the sharp outline of a rim. He estimated its diameter to be about 50 feet.

Knowing how excited his wife and son would be, Amy called to them as he ran toward the house, and they came out in time to marvel at the strange craft as it proceeded smoothly on toward the eastern ridge of mountains.

"It headed toward that peak over there," Amy said, pointing to the ridge about a mile away. "It climbed up a little as it got closer, and just about that time the front light went out, so there were only two lights when it got to the peak and went behind it. When it came out the other side, there was only one light, not much bigger than a star that it passed."

Remembering a friend in nearby Windermere who was skeptical of UFO stories, Amy went in to phone and tell him just where to look. When he returned outside, the light had stopped moving.

"It looked so much like the star next to it that Elizabeth and I began to wonder if we had been seeing things," he said. "We went back in the house and about 15 minutes later my son Arnold came in, too. He said the light was still there.

But Amy's friend in Windermere kept watching to settle this UFO business once and for all. When he started looking, the light was stationary. But after a few minutes, as he said later, it started to move. First it sped northward at a fast clip, then it crossed the valley and headed south, passing close to his house where he had a good look at it.

Thus another convert was won!

* * *

An astonishing sign that UFOs are interested in the precise contours of the Rocky Mountain Trench was provided in the spring of 1963. The witnesses were Mrs. Katherine Beamish and Mrs. Barbara Baker, at the time both of Edgewater, B.C.

When the incident occurred the two were driving toward Radium just before the morning work traffic had started.

"Suddenly we both noticed a brilliant light in the air which we thought must be just about over the hot-springs pool," Mrs. Beamish said. "It was so intensely bright it was hard to look at it. But we shaded our eyes to look, we were so excited. It was far more brilliant than the sun."

As the two continued slowly ahead the light seemed to take on still more brilliance, and at this point appeared to release another object from its far side.

"This one had a whitish opaque appearance, something like a cloud, but its outline was very sharp and it was completely round," Mrs. Beamish said. "It looked simply like a huge ball."

While the brilliant parent body held its position, the second object started to move toward the mountain peaks a mile or so in the background. These peaks form the eastern ridge of the Trench and, to a person looking from a good vantage point at Radium, disappear to the south almost at the international border.

As soon as the ball-shaped body reached the summit it started an amazing performance as if the gods were having a gigantic game on their Olympian heights.

"It looked to us as if this enormous ball was bouncing from one peak to another—bouncing, bouncing," Mrs. Beamish said, with a movement of her head. "It seemed to be touching the very tips of the mountains, and it went bouncing along so gracefully until it disappeared far to the south. If I had been alone I might have been skeptical and thought it was an illusion. But my friend was excited, too. We discussed it after and agreed we had both seen exactly the same thing. It was a very thrilling experience.

While is was difficult to judge time during such a stunning spectacle, Mrs. Beamish figured it lasted "not more than 10 minutes." She said the ball at no time moved out over the valley but stayed unerringly over the Rocky Mountain ridge curving slightly inward to the south. Meanwhile, at some unnoticed stage, the brilliant light over the pool faded out as if finished with its part in this playtime of the gods.

As our visit was ending, Mrs. Beamish remembered one more incident which may or may not have been connected with the main event. She rose and pointed to a section of the same ridge of mountains visible from her window.

"Just before we left that morning we saw something that looked like a parachute coming down right over there. We thought it was odd because there wasn't a plane in sight and we hadn't heard one."

STAR GODS, HOPI REVELATIONS AND THE MISSING SACRED STONE

Tucson's Chris Warner has long had a special linkage with the Amerindian tribes of the South West, often visiting Second Mesa in Arizona to consult with the medicine men. She realizes the importance the Hopi—as well as various other tribes—play in both the visitation of Earth by extraterrestrial beings as well as the fact that we may be entering the Last Days of the current cycle of civilization on Earth. Her own dramatic encounters along with those of her close friend and associate Jackie Blue illustrate how these matters have touched the hearts and souls of many in an increasing manner. This is Chris's story.

In January, 1985, I had a most unusual and vivid dream. In this dream I was driving along a stretch of highway in the desert area of Arizona on an Indian reservation. Exactly which reservation it was I couldn't tell.

It was dusk, and as I was driving along heading west, I saw a rather large group of Indians walking off to the right side of the road. They appeared to be on a pilgrimage. Instinctively, I stopped the car and began walking with them. I sensed this was sacred ground and this pilgrimage was to be conducted on foot. I was accepted by the Indians as if I were one of them. We continued west, and after walking for what seemed like a couple of hours we looked up into the sky towards the north and saw a brilliant object coming out of a cluster of stars and heading straight for us. The object alternated in color white to red and back again. When it was about a mile above us it zipped heavenward and melted back into the constellation from which it came. To the Indians, this did not seem unusual and they did not get frightened or alarmed.

We continued our walk and by morning we arrived at the top of a mesa. By then I had progressed to the front of the group. A lone pinion plant decorated the top of this mesa. A medicine man and their chief were present. Our attention was turned toward the sky and a large UFO was coming down.

I began praying very fervently at this point.

"Oh God," I said, "if this is a sign of peace to come let a white dove land on my arm." Instead of one white dove, two white doves proceeded out of the clouds and landed on my arm.

My attention was then focused on the sky where a huge eagle about the size of a passenger jet was flying from east to west. Strangely enough, it had a white bear, (not a polar bear) and a deer riding atop its back.

At this point I woke up, but the dream was so vivid I have never forgotten it. In fact, it was so life-like that I called Dan and Aileen Edwards, directors of a group called the UFO Contact Center in Seattle, Washington.

"Sounds like you should be taking a trip down to the Hopi reservation," Dan commented during out conversation.

"Why?" I was anxious to know.

He responded, "We have been doing much work with the Hopi lately, and they are very much into UFOs."

To assist in my quest, he gave me a list of names of who to contact if I decided to go to the reservation.

A little while later, I called Dottie Burrow, a long time friend of mine in Laramie, and also of Dr. R. Leo Sprinkle from the University of Wyoming at Laramie. I relayed my dream to her and her response was nearly the same as Dan Edwards' had been.

"I've also been drawn to the Hopi lately," she said. "I have been working with a medicine woman and we're heading there ourselves next month. Why don't you come with us?"

Unfortunately, due to my duties and obligations as a mother, I had to decline until arrangements could be made later on for me to make such a trip.

At this point, I contacted my close friend, Jackie Blue, founder of the Center for UFO Studies in Glenwood Springs, Colorado, and told her of the dream and the way it seemed to be tying in with the experiences of other UFO contactees.

"Something definitely seems to be going on!" she remarked, "Do you feel as if you are being drawn to the Hopi?" she asked.

"It sure seems that way," was my sincere response.

"OK, then," she said, "let's make a tentative date to go there and find out what this is all about!"

We decided on the end of May since the kids would be out of school and we could take them with us if necessary. Since it was still March we had a while to plan. We kept in touch with Dan Edwards, and it was during the course of one of our conversations that he asked me if I knew "anything about the double-eagle symbol."

"No, never heard of it. What does it mean?" I was curious to find out.

"Well," he said, "there is a legend pertaining to two alien bodies in suspended animation somewhere in Arizona. When the time is right these bodies will awaken and command a fleet of ships buried somewhere in central Arizona. These two beings are known as eagles or commanders," he continued.

"I have had several dreams of eagles," I thoughtfully noted. "I have seen myself turn into an eagle. I've seen a pure white eagle, a turquoise eagle, and another eagle as big as a house."

Then Dan wanted to know something else. "Have you had any dreams about finding a rock?"

At first I thought, "No, not really." Then I remembered a dream within the previous two months.

In the dream I found myself wandering out in the desert with a UFO hovering above me. I seemed to be able to see right through it. There were a lot of people on board. . . people who looked just like us! They were urging me to find a stone. I didn't understand at first, but they kept prodding me to look under this particular rock which was dish-shaped and rather heavy. I pushed it over and scraped away the sand and there was this flat sandstone rock, kind of round on one side and broken on the other. It has a six pointed star carved on it.

"Then what happened?" Edwards asked, eager to hear the rest of my story.

"Then the ship came down and they let me inside. They took the rock, which seemed to have some power to it. They told me they had been waiting a long time to return, but could not until the stone had been recovered. I asked them why, if they knew where the stone was all the time, didn't they just come and get it. They replied, 'Because the time is not of our choosing.' They said that when mankind recovered the stone he would be ready for the New World. They also told me that they had lived here before, but left and since then had been waiting for the signal to return.

"Then what happened?" Dan wanted to know.

"Then I woke up," I had to admit, saddened that it had been cut off like this.

Still, Dan was noticeably elated. "Do you know of the story of the Bahana, the White Brother who possesses half of the stone tablet and who is supposed to return someday bearing the stone at the beginning of the New Age?"

"Never heard of it." I had to be honest.

"This is incredible!" he exclaimed. "You need to get the book *Fourth World of the Hopi.* Get it right away."

I found the book at the local library and began reading. It tells of the Hopi coming out of their last civilization or Third World. As they begin their long journey in a new land or the Fourth World, they split into groups or clans. At the time the Bahana or White Brother was with them. As the Bahana went on their separate path, the chief took a flat piece of stone and carved a picture on it. What the drawing consisted of is not clear. The chief then took the stone and broke it in two pieces, retaining a portion and giving the other portion to the Bahana. When someday the Bahana returned with the missing portion, it would signify the entering into the Fifth World or, as we know it, the New Age.

Jackie Blue and I left for our trip on May 31, 1985. We drove all day. When we were about seventy miles from the Hopi reservation, still in the heart of Navajo land, we lost the muffler off the van and it caught on the rear left tire. We panicked! Just then a brown van pulled up from behind. A cowboy got out. A real Billy Jack!

"Looks like you ladies need some help," he said.

As I sat there drooling, Jackie explained to the man that it was a brand new muffler. "I can't imagine why it came off like that," she said, trying to make conversation. He examined the van and temporarily secured the broken piece.

"It won't hold very long," he said. "You need to get it fixed right away."

"Great," I whispered to Jackie, "there isn't a garage within two hundred miles!."

Then the man who introduced himself as Mike said, "if you just drive it over across the highway there to that metal building, I'll weld it for you."

Jackie was afraid. "Where's the gun?" she asked.

"In the bag," I replied. I always carried it with me on trips—snakes, you know. We drove over to the building and Mike met us there.

"Bring it inside," he said.

We drove the van in and Mike began working on it. About that time a Navajo lady came in with her two small children. She introduced herself as Mike's wife. We had brought children's clothing with us and invited her to help herself if she needed anything.

"I hope he takes Master Charge," I whispered to Jackie. "I'll bet this costs at least a couple hundred."

I was feeling sick at the thought.

"Will you take a credit card?" I asked as Mike finished up.

"There's no charge," he looked right through us. "Just pass it on down the road."

We couldn't believe it! This man possessed a genuine kind of human compassion. It was as if we were being protected by some unseen force. This stranger had just been there at the right time in the middle of the desert. If he hadn't been there we could have been stuck under the hot sun for days!

We thanked Mike sincerely. How could we ever forget such a lesson in trust and love! We went on our way and arrived at the edge of the Hopi reservation just after dark. At the border the van sputtered and died at the same time a yellowish-green light passed over our vehicle. It lasted only a couple of seconds.

Did you see that?!" Jackie exclaimed.

"What was it, can you tell?" I asked.

"It's gone, whatever it was," Jackie stammered.

We arrived at the Hopi Cultural Center in New Oraibi, Arizona later that evening. The next morning we went looking for some of the contacts referred to us by Dan and Aileen. The first house we arrived at was that of Stanley and Nora. Stanley claims the position of chief, although there is dispute among the Hopi as to who is really their leader. It seems that Stanley was the adopted son of the late chief who preceded him. Hopi law says the successor must be a blood relative.

Stanley was not at home, but his wife, Nora, let us in and we talked with her. We brought fresh fruit as a gift, including a pineapple which she really enjoyed.

I told Nora of my dreams. She was absolutely fascinated with the part about the vision of the eagle, the bear, and the deer.

We asked Nora about the stone and if she knew of it.

"My husband has the original piece," she claimed. "It has been in his family since the very beginning."

"Can we see it?" I asked.

"No one can see it," she said. "Not even I have seen it. Only the men have seen it. You must go see the medicine man Augustine and tell him of your dreams. You can find him at Second Mesa."

She gave us the directions and after a very frustrating couple of hours of driving

To this day many Amerindian tribes tell tales around the campfire of visitors from the stars.

around, we found him planting in a field with his sons and grandsons.

I coaxed one of his young grandsons over and tried to convince him to get his grandfather. It appeared the youngster didn't speak a word of English. So by pointing to his grandfather the lad finally figured out what we wanted. Augustine came over to us.

"We were sent to you by Nora. I need to talk to you."

"Wait for me," he said.

He went back to leave instructions with the others. Then he rejoined us.

"Take me home," he said. "I show you."

His English was not too good. I just hoped he could understand us. We arrived at a small, meager hut.

"Here," he said.

He took us inside. There on a shelf was a statue of the white bear!

"Look, Jackie," I was tickled pink. "There's the white bear from my dream!"

Augustine asked us to sit. "Why are you here?" he wanted to know.

Once again I found myself relating the story. When I got to the part about the eagle, the bear, and the deer, his eyes grew bright. When I finished he said to us, "Come, I show you something." With this, he took us to a small prayer room off the living room. Mounted on the wall was a deer head, decorated in exquisite turquoise.

"That is my God Father. You may pray for guidance."

We did as he said. He pulled back a curtain and revealed an eagle kachina the likes of which I have never seen.

"This is my God symbol," he told us. "You were wise to follow your dream. The white bear is my clan. You have been sent to me. Come now, I make you a Hopi."

He took us back to the living room. He produced some eagle feathers, pahohs (prayer sticks), and other religious paraphernalia. He began chanting and then said, "Now I make you well."

At the time, I was having pain in my left hip. I never let on, nor did I tell him about it. I mentioned it to Jackie earlier in the day so she already knew about it. What we saw next absolutely amazed us! Augustine reached into the left pocket of my jeans and pulled and pinched and finally yanked out some gray matter which came right through the material of my pants! Then he simply tossed it into the fireplace.

"You have asthma since a child," he told me. "You have problems with your lungs, too."

He was correct on both counts. Then he told me, "You have bad heart. If you not come to me you would die."

Well, even though I never had this problem diagnosed, I knew I was prone to having an irregular heartbeat at times. From each of these areas he would either pull out gray matter or something that looked like a small stone. It was incredible!

"There are people who wish evil on you. That is why you are sick," he went on to explain the cause of my condition.

When he was finished with me he did the same thing to Jackie. When he was done with us, we had some pretty bad bruises, but we didn't let on that it hurt.

Finally I asked him, "Why did I see a UFO?"

"What?" he asked.

"UFO," I repeated. "Why did I see a ship come down out of the sky?"

"Forget you see it," he said almost angrily. "You need not know. It is not important for you to know."

It was as if we had overwhelmed him with that question. It seemed we had touched upon something sacred within the Hopi realm and we dared not intrude.

"You Hopi now, what clan are you?" he asked us.

Jackie and I both hesitated.

"You belong to spider clan," he told Jackie.

"Yuk," I said, "I hate spiders."

"What clan you choose?" he asked me.

"I don't know," I said, a bit bewildered by all of this.

At the time I was fidgeting with a six pointed star necklace I was wearing around my neck.

"You belong to star clan," Augustine said, holding my necklace in his hand. "Take me back now. I give you medicine."

We drove him back to the field.

While we waited for him, we gave some clothing to his grandchildren who flocked around us.

A few minutes later Augustine came back with a jar of Hopi tea made out of desert plants.

"Take this three times a day, this much," indicating the proper dosage. "Take some now."

It tasted like weak iodine, but not too bad. Finally we thanked him and left.

Though we originally had planned to stay three days, we decided at the last minute to leave for Sedona, Arizona.

We took the medicine for a couple of days and noticed that is was having a mild tranquilizing effect on us.

"Do you think we should drink this stuff?" I asked Jackie at our campsite just below Sedona.

"I don't know, do you think we should get rid of it?" she asked.

"Let's ask for a sign," I said. "If we're supposed to drink this stuff, let a rabbit cross right in front of the van." "Oh heck," I continued. "No rabbit is going to cross here. We haven't seen a rabbit the whole trip."

So we dumped the stuff out. Just then, a rabbit crossed right in front of the van where I said it should. We just looked at each other.

It seems as though through the dreams I had, a whole new realm opened up to us. The symbols fitted exactly into place when we were led to Augustine. And what of Mike, the friendly cowboy who happened to be at the right place at the right time. Was something trying to stop us from our purpose and yet something good intervened as it always seems to do if you give it a chance? Was it pure chance he happened to be there out in the middle of four hundred square miles of desert? And what of the lesson we learned? We were mistrusting, and this man showed us faith in humankind.

But, of course, the main question is why we were led to the Hopi. I think that question will be answered for all of us in the future in the New Age. From what

I've come to understand, our spiritual brother, the American Indian, will play an important part in our finding a safe haven at the time global disaster strikes. The Hopi have many prophecies which tell of grave dangers due to mankind's negativity, his misuse of the planet, and his generally destructive ways. Many tribal legends make reference to God-like beings from the Stars who landed openly in eons past to share their wisdom and knowledge with the redman. It is said these spiritually advanced Souls are about to return in greater numbers than ever before and will renew their longstanding friendship with our Native Americans.

Isn't it apparent that the Indians have an important message to impart to all of us, and isn't it about time we listened?

THE MYSTERIOUS "STAR SYMBOL" OF THE UFONAUTS — WHAT COULD BE ITS SACRED MEANING?

Since several of my articles on UFOs and their involvement with the American Indian appeared in the UFO Review I have recalled other significant events which may have important bearing on explaining to readers why keeping a journal of their experiences is important. Though I am lax at keeping records myself, I urge all of you to start a diary and keep it up to date.

On February 28, 1981, I met with Dr. Leo Sprinkle, Professor of Psychology from the University of Wyoming, at my residence in Black Hawk, Colorado. He conducted a hypnosis session which re-sulted in some big changes in my life. I had been having perplexing dreams and coincidental occurrences that I had hoped Leo could help me with.

In one dream (which I consider to be the most important in my search for the star symbol), I was walking along a street in a small, old western town, somewhere in northern Colorado or southern Wyoming. There was a corner brick building which housed the local tavern, and my attention quickly focused on the entrance to this establishment. In the dream, I witnessed three drunken cowboys dragging what appeared to be a small alien being the size of a four year old child out to the street where they shot the creature with a rifle. I became enraged at the event taking place and I said something to the men which made them flee in terror. (I wish I could remember what it was!). I picked up and cradled the small creature, and in his pain he said, "Take me to where the star is." I looked up to the evening sky and wondered, "How in the hell am I going to get up there?" The small alien, obviously was disturbed at my thinking and said to me, "That's not the only kind of star. Look around you."

As I looked around the street, I saw a small cafe with a Star of David over the doorway. I remember it as being a black outlined star against a white background. I took the little guy inside and when I reached the doorway, a tall, lean man ushered me immediately inside, took the small creature from my arms and placed him on a water-bed in the rear of the cafe. I remember worrying about him because the bed started sloshing around which made him uncomfortable. The man then took him underground to a complex that I was not allowed to see.

The following transcript from my hypnotic regression session with Dr. Sprinkle contains further insights:

Sprinkle: (Suggestions to review other questions.)

Warner: I wish to talk about the place of the star.

Sprinkle: Go ahead.

Warner: I feel the place is not here ... the star is a symbol. It's a dark star on a white background.

Sprinkle: Do you have any impressions?

Warner: The symbol represents a race of beings that some of us are to work with. Some people follow certain symbols, some of us follow others. This symbol is being given to me so I will be aware of it and be ready.

Sprinkle: Is there any other information about this star?

Warner: Not now.

Sprinkle: Is there any other information at this time?

Warner: I would like to discuss the two points of light I keep seeing in my dreams. I have been there before, to a planet which had two suns.

Sprinkle: Is there a name for this place?

Warner: I don't know it.

Sprinkle: Can you give more information about this place?

Warner: I have been there before, to a planet of one of the suns. I lived there, I was taught there, It was a place where life was peaceful, very good, only something happened, like a war or conflict. No,

it was different. A catastrophe of some kind.

Sprinkle: Is this important?

Warner: Yes, something happened. I'll become aware.

Sprinkle: (Suggestions to go back to that lifetime) Are you ready now?

Warner: Okay, I'm ready now. At the time of the catastrophe, I was a pilot. My job was to go from the planet to a moon mining station. I remember looking out a very large window and seeing a yellow planet very close to the gravitational field of our own planet. As the planets circled each of the suns and each other, this other planet would be pulled closer to our own because of our stronger gravitational pull. This would be the last time. Evacuation was ready. The planets will collide. I remember getting children aboard a long cylindrical craft. We were getting ready to take off. People were begging, crying and screaming to get aboard. We were all crying. I didn't want to leave anyone behind but there was no choice. My job was to take the children to a new colony elsewhere.

Sprinkle: Was this earth?

Warner: I don't know.

Sprinkle: (Suggestions for a deeper trance state) Do you wish to give any other information at this time?

Warner: (Seeing as both participant and observer) I remember seeing three people, from a past life perhaps. I remember them sitting above me like three judges. They were wearing dull colored robes with hoods. I asked them, "Who was I in my past life?"

They didn't like my question and are reluctant to answer. "Please!" I beg them. "I have to know!" One of them says okay and takes me by the hand. (Immediately I see myself as a small, young blonde girl. I am in a room with a cement floor, and there is a young boy here who I think is my brother.)

There are three soldiers here with guns. One of them is saying to me, "You are a Jew. You must die!"

"No," I insist, "I'm not a Jew!"

"You are a Jew!" the man screams. "Your father was a Jew! You must die!"

The man aims a rifle at me and shoots me in the abdomen. At this point during hypnosis, I experience the pain as vividly as if the event were actually taking place.

I watched as my intestines spilled forth onto the floor and I can feel the tearing, burning pain. Eventually numbness begins to take over and I black out.

The next thing I recall is a tall blond man in the room who takes me by the hand and leads me outside to a waiting UFO. Inside I again see the three robed figures and then one of them says to me, "Remember the name *Shasa Kelly*."

An astute reader can immediately see the attachment to the Star, as the Jews are associated with the Star of David. The name Shasa Kelly is significant. Perhaps someday I will come across it again.

Shortly after this hypnotic session with Dr. Sprinkle, I met Pat McGuire, a Wyoming rancher who claimed to be having an ongoing series of UFO contacts. After seeing his story on the television show, "That's incredible." I called Leo on the phone and practically screamed at him.

"Why didn't you tell me about this man? You knew about him all the time," I raised my voice frantically. Dr. Sprinkle had hypnotized Pat right on the air.

Pat McGuire claimed that alien beings came to his practically hidden ranch on the Wyoming plains regularly. He was urged by them to fly the Israeli flag on his ranch, a flag that has on it the Star of David. A dark star on a light background. I knew this was the symbol I was supposed to be watching for!

Leo's reply to me, "You had to find out for yourself."

I met Pat McGuire shortly after the Second Annual Rocky Mountain UFO Conference at Laramie. Pat and I became friends immediately as his personality is most magnetic. He took me out to his ranch where I spent the next couple of days.

That summer I worked with Pat at the Black Cat Fireworks Company out of Rawlins, Wyoming, delivering fireworks all over the state. Several times we seemed to lose all sense of time, and some trips even took longer than they should have. But it wasn't until we drove south to Rawlins from Buffalo, Wyoming that we noticed that a four-hour trip took only about two and a half hours. Now things were starting to become really bizarre! No way had I been driving 160 miles an hour! That night as we left Rawlins at about 11:00 P.M., heading east for Laramie with another load of fireworks, I noticed three unusually bright stars ahead and I commented to Pat about how beautiful they were.

Just then the middle star began to "fall" our way at an incredible rate of speed. I remember yelling to Pat, "It's going to hit us!" But it stopped short, causing Pat to almost lose control of the trunk and swerve over to the shoulder. The star on the let was now proceeding north and we noticed through a pair of binoculars that an Air Force jet was giving pursuit. When the jet caught up with the object, the object sped off, leaving the jet as if it were just sitting there.

The star to our right proceeded north also, leaving the huge star "light" in front of us as if it were trying to tell us something. Within a few minutes it also disappeared into nothingness as if someone just flipped off a light switch.It was an incredible, fulfilling phenomena that I'll remember the rest of my life.

This all took place in 1981. As you may remember from my last article, when I visited the Hopi reservation in 1985 I was initiated into the star clan of the Hopi by the tribe's medicine man. This all certainly seems to mean something. Perhaps I am following an invisible trail of some kind. Since then, I have enrolled in college and I am now taking a course in Animal Health Technology (Veterinarian Tech) in which, so far, I am a straight A student. It seems that I am interested in working with the Hopi at least in so far as my internship goes. Perhaps I will end up working with other members of the "star clan" as well.

While attending college I am living nearby on a beautiful secluded ranch site. Recently, I discovered there were two wolverines on the ranch which is very unusual in this part of the country—so much so that there has not been a wolverine sighted here in several years. Wolverines are a sacred Indian symbol denoting bravery and cunning, and are symbolic of warriors. Wolverines are considered powerful medicine among many tribes.

UFOs have also been sighted all around here and the place has a magical aura about it. It is a good retreat for getting away and keeping in touch with nature. There are nearby hot springs, rafting on the Colorado River, skiing at Aspen, beautiful mountain lakes and rivers, and the ranch site itself sits on a natural wildlife habitat in full view of beautiful Mt. Sopris (itself a sacred mountain among the Utes).[1] I have a feeling that other incredible things are going to happen around here and I will be part of them.

Jackie Blue, founder of the Center for UFO Studies in Glenwood Springs, Colorado.

45

DO HOPI PROPHECIES HOLD KEY TO MYSTERIOUS ARTIFACT?

Though we think of pyramids normally in terms of being constructed in Egypt, such structures actually ring the world. In Mexico, for example, the pyramids there had great spiritual significance to the Mayans who were the first great mathematicians, putting up observatories and actually working their dating system into the stones and angles of their pyramids. Now a new discovery threatens to prove that we are in the "Last Days," and that the Amerindians are to play an important role in the cleansing period that will soon engulf our Earth Mother.

An unusual discovery of a strange artifact made halfway around the world has led an Australian woman to meet with representatives of an American Indian tribe in hopes of obtaining some answers linked to the origin and meaning of a mysterious 92 lb. rock showing a sun symbol and two serpents carved into one side.

On March 25, 1982, Marilyn Pye of Queensland was told while attending a psychic channeling session that a "golden pyramid" existed ninety miles north of Cairns, Australia. Within five weeks, Marilyn had sold her home, walked out of a newly opened business and retained the help of a well-known New York psychic, Bryce Bond, to help her unlock the secret of these pyramids, which, at first, Australian archaeologists refused to acknowl-

edge the mere existence of. Responding to nationwide media coverage, Marilyn was led to the town of Toowoomba, Queensland, where a strange basalt crystal rock was unearthed beneath 24 feet of soil. Quite easily it was determined that this stone and its peculiar writing was *not* the work of aboriginal natives, though legends of the local tribes do tell of not one but two "golden pyramids" in the near vicinity of this remarkable scientific find.

Packing the 92 lb. artifact in a special crate, Marilyn flew with her "precious cargo" first to Hawaii to meet with the Kahuna who did a reading on the rock. They concluded that the engraving had been done 30,000 years ago with three different sized laser beams. They also said the rock was a "computer" which could be

Marilyn Pye of Queensland, Australia poses with mysterious artifact which Hopi Indians say may hold clue to its origin.   Photo by Tim Beckley.

used to bring wisdom and peace to the world.

At this stage in her quest, Marilyn became aware of the Hopi prophecies concerning the return of the true white brother, which tells of a white person bringing the symbol of the sun to the Hopi. The Kahuna said there were three other rocks, while a Hopi representative told Marilyn that several engraved rocks exist on different continents and that they must come forth before the day of purification.

Marilyn sensed that she had to meet with the Hopi. Four days after arriving in New York, she was introduced to John Hill, an Iroguoi Indian who was in Manhattan to speak at the United Nations regarding the "last days" which many Indians feel are approaching.

When Marilyn showed Mr. Hill the rock, he became very excited and arranged for many important people to view the artifact while Marilyn remained in the city. The effect on people was amazing. The rock seemed to be putting out incredibly beautiful energy. People would become light and very energized. Through a chain of events, the Hopi found out about the rock and were anxious to determine if it was indeed the missing rock of their prophecies.

Six days before Christmas, Marilyn decided to travel to Arizona where she would meet with Medicine Men familiar with such religious and spiritual matters.

As can sometimes happen on cross-country jaunts, the journey turned into a nightmare. Planes were delayed. Flights were missed. Connections got crossed, but finally Marilyn and a Peruvian Indian traveling with her arrived at their destination. They both felt that some supernatural power was trying to prevent them from getting the rock to the Hopi.

It had been arranged for Marilyn to meet with Grandfather David, who is over 100 years old and blind. He felt the rock's engraving and became very excited. "This is what we have been waiting for. There are three others to come," is all he would say. Marilyn was asked to leave the rock behind so that the Hopi priests could take a closer look at it.

The rock was returned to her six days later, after the Hopi had taken a rubbing of the artifact's surface to determine its origin and meaning. To date, the Hopi have remained tight lipped about their findings, which has convinced Ms. Pye all the more that there is something to her startling discovery.

The story of the rock is apparently far from over. Marilyn clearly believes that there is much more to be said about this ROCK OF AGES, and is now trying to get government support in her native Australia to dig for the "golden pyramid(s)," which she is convinced exist(s) in Australia and may have origins dating back thousands of years to a previous civilization that may have existed on this planet long before the time of Noah's flood. There is reason to believe the Hopi could help her unravel the pieces of this cosmic jigsaw puzzle.

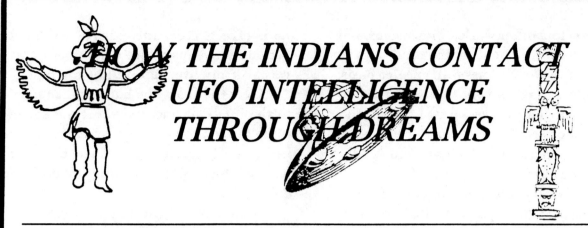

HOW THE INDIANS CONTACT UFO INTELLIGENCE THROUGH DREAMS

In many cultures dreams play an important role in prophetic visions. Going back to the Christian Bible, there are many references made to this very theme, and entire nations have literally been known to change hands *overnight* due to some form of nocturnal symbolism. The Amerindians were quite knowledgeable when it came to their dreams, seeing great importance in them. In the next several pages, reporter Chris Warner, who has visited and studied extensively with several of Arizona's most influential medicine men, offers her own personal experiences and findings on this most intriguing topic and how it relates to the UFO-Amerindian lineage.

I n previous chapters I described in detail my dream about the American Indians as related to UFOs and predictions involving the so-called "End Times" or "Last Days." In my second piece for Tim Beckley's *UFO Review*, I indicated that I thought some dreams were not just "dreams" but had special significance, especially to those of us who tend to be sensitive or psychic by nature.

Never in my wildest imagination did I suspect that my article would generate such reader response. Over a period of a few months, I have received mail from all over the United States, Canada, and from several foreign countries indicating that I was not alone in my seemingly unusual beliefs. From what I was being told, many people have recently found their dreams serving as a springboard for heightened states of awareness. One Houston, Texas man said every night while he slept he was being trained in higher mathematics for a purpose which he did not fully understand, but which would become clear to him in the next few months. A woman from Hollywood, Florida wrote to say that she had been taken on board a mile long mothership several times and was given the power to heal. Both readers were mystified over how higher intelligences were using the dream state to literally get into their minds.

During numerous trips to the Hopi Reservation in Arizona, I have discussed the process of dreaming with several Indian medicine men. One in particular, a kind gentleman named Augustine, confessed that to the Hopi dreams have always been a sacred way of communication with the "other side," especially in times of great tribulation. Apparently, beings from other worlds, dimensions, and realms find this one of the best ways to communicate with us on an ongoing basis. And now that many of us are starting to have our Third Eye opened, more and more such seemingly strange occurrences will take place while we are supposedly "sound asleep."

Naturally, not all dreams are of a psychic nature, but some definitely are, and this has even been proved in several instances.

Take, for example, the case of the 38-year-old RN who poured her heart out to UFO writer and investigator Brad Steiger. I sat spellbound along with UFO Review publisher Timothy Green Beckley and movie producer/writer Sherry Hanson, as "Janet" (not her real name) related an experience that took place some eight or nine years ago along a lonely stretch of Utah roadway.

According to this very practical career woman, she was riding with a girlfriend when they stopped to pick up a hitchhiker—something they would absolutely never do under normal circumstances.

"There was just something so compelling about him that we couldn't do anything but pull over and let him into our car," Janet explained.

The next thing they remember is pulling into Janet's driveway near Phoenix. "A period of time had elapsed and while we were hundreds of miles from home when we last stopped, we didn't seem to have used very much gas."

In reality—as it turned out—*three entire days* had gone by. "We could not recall anything that transpired. It was as if we had a mental block." And while Janet's friend seemed to have suffered no ill-effects from the experience, Janet became very upset and very uneasy. "It was as if my life were falling apart."

Over the years she had told her story to absolutely no one, and yet it was something she could not easily forget. Little by little, she began to remember bits and pieces which were starting to emerge during her dream state.

"I remember picking up the stranger and driving for a while until we came to a side road which we turned off onto. The road lead to a clearing where a strange disc-shaped craft was resting. My girlfriend and I were ushered onboard by the hitchhiker who kept repeating that he meant us no harm. There were other people inside the ship and they all went about their duties as if we weren't there."

During the course of the time she spent onboard, Janet asked why they had selected her and she was told by the alien being that it was because she was the one who "held the key."

"I kept telling them that I didn't know what they were talking about . . . that I didn't have any 'key,' but they just kept shaking their head and insisting I did, and that I would find out what they were talking about when the 'time is right.'"

Attempting to get on with her life, Janet tried her best to push these dreams out of her mind, but they would still take place from time to time, and always featured the same "man" she had picked up at the roadside. Several years after the experience, Janet got married and in due process had a baby girl. One night when the child was about six years old she woke up screaming. "I ran into her bed

Chris Warner stands with Medicine Man Augustine who revealed inner meaning of dreams to the Oracle, Arizona researcher.

room as this behavior was so unlike her. My little girl was crying 'Mommie, Mommie, they're in the house and they want to see you. They say they've come *for the key*!'"

To say the least, Janet was flabbergasted because here was additional proof that her experience was not just a figment of her imagination. "I had never told my daughter about the man in the craft, my dream, or anything to do with my experience, and here she was repeating the same phrase to me that I had been told directly. Somehow they had gotten to my daughter in her dreams to pass on a message to me."

Janet says she still has no idea what they want or why they picked her, and she isn't one hundred percent sure she wants to find out.

Sometime back I had a somewhat parallel experience happen to me though it didn't directly involve missing time.

Three years ago I was warned by an unknown figure in a dream that if I left my husband my son would become temporarily blinded in an accident due to events that would follow after my separation. During the dream, I asked the entity to spare my son.

"Please," I begged, "let me take his place. Don't let him suffer!"

On June 16, 1985, I left my husband and moved in with a man by the name of Robin who had been my horse shoer. I needed a place to stay, and being broke at the time, had no other alternatives. Robin and I grew very fond of each other. He was also recently separated and we found some comfort in each other's misery.

During a trip we made together to Colorado, we came across two quarter-horses for sale that we were very much interested in. One was a tall, boxy horse, well built and lean. The other was a stout, heavy muscled zebra dun. The dun was a real beauty and I decided to buy him for Robin as a gift. We named the tall, lean, red horse Roger and the dun we named Buck. And so Buck and Roger came home with us to our small town of Black Hawk, Colorado.

We soon found that the horses could not be separated. I had a fear of horses because of an earlier accident, so Robin began working with Roger to make sure he was safe for me to ride. Unfortunately, whenever Roger was taken out of the pasture, Buck would go crazy. He would run up and down the fence line, ready to charge the barbed wire at any given moment. "Please tie him up. He's going to go through the fence!" I pleaded more than once.

Robin tried tying him to one of the posts in the barn, but Buck was so strong that he broke the post and almost caused the barn roof to collapse on top of him.

"This is not going to work," I said. "We need something much stronger."

The next day, I went and bought two strong nylon halters and a heavy duty bull rope. We tied Buck up with both halters and strung the rope to a nearby telephone pole. He fought so violently that at first I thought he was going to break his neck. After several lessons Buck finally settled down. Robin decided then that it would be all right not to have to tie Buck up anymore. I wasn't so sure.

On August 16th, Robin, my son Dusty, and I went to the pasture so Robin could continue training Roger. Robin rode around the outside of the fence with

Buck merrily following along, while my car was parked on the road next to the barbed wire fence. Just on the inside of the fence near my car was a small pond which was about twelve feet deep. Robin rode past me and the car, and when Buck tried to follow, he came to the pond and panicked. The horse tried to jump the fence and entangled his back legs in the attempt! In his pain he became a dangerous runaway locomotive.

I was standing behind my car with the trunk lid up. I began yelling at Robin frantically. He was barely within hearing range.

"Look out!" I yelled to him. "Buck went through the fence." I heard the barbed wire whistling in the air. I could hear it getting caught and snapping free like an overstretched rubber band. Things began to move in slow motion.

Dusty was standing next to me. The remaining barbed wire strand was just on the other side of him. Buck had reached the car by now and was just running past trying to get to Roger, his buddy whom he thought would save him. I could hear the wire whipping through the air. I knocked Dusty to the ground and the wire missed him, but it caught on the hood ornament of my car and sprang loose catching me across the eyes and throat. It felt like all the bones in my face had been smashed. My throat felt constricted. I knew my trachea had been damaged. I lay on the ground in agony. The reaction of my son and boyfriend were oblivious to me.

"I always wondered how I was going to die," I thought. As I was lying there gasping for air, I heard a voice say to me, "Just calm down, you're not going to die."

Buck had taken out 400 feet of wire and two solid posts. I was certainly lucky to be breathing. Robin rushed me to the emergency room of the nearest hospital which was 30 miles away. He gave me a handkerchief to cover my face. My wounds were unbearable. I was sleepy and I could barely breathe. My lungs had started to swell. I tried to swallow but couldn't. I started to choke and I was in shock.

When I got to the hospital, I was lifted out of the car and put on a stretcher. I drifted in and out of consciousness. I remember at one point talking to the entity who had warned me about the accident.

"I spared your son," he said. "That's all I could do. You will be all right, you will live," the being continued.

The doctors pulled the rag off my face. I heard one of the nurses gasp. As I tried to look up I could see only white light.

It was like trying to look through a glass of milk. It took 60 stitches around my eyes. I was bandaged like a mummy. When my condition stabilized the doctors explained to me that night that the retina on both of my eyes had been torn loose from the impact of the blow. They told me my chances of ever seeing again were 50-50. I could see the doctor was not optimistic.

When I started to cry, the doctor got very upset. "Don't cry. Don't sneeze. Don't cough. Don't even get up to go to the bathroom or your eyes will start to hemorrhage again."

For almost three weeks I lay in bed. Robin stayed by my side the whole time tending to my every need. Finally, slowly my sight returned. The blinding had only been temporary as told to me by the entity in my dream, which I am convinced was a message from another loving consciousness not of this world.

Many people are prone to believe that most dreams are not very significant. . . that events of the day may have triggered meaningless labyrinths of garbled pictures or perhaps they are the mind's bizarre correlations of trying to make sense—or nonsense—out of life's daily challenges.

But people do not pay attention to the fact that while in an altered state of consciousness our "higher self" is exposed nightly to outside influences, and that during this state, higher intelligences may be able to make contact with us.

These dream in which warnings or messages are given may in reality be of greater significance than ordinary dreams, and can be placed in the category of visions. Often, these types of "dreams" are more vivid and seem more real than ordinary dreams. Frequently such visions arrive in the form of symbols, leaving us to decipher the true meanings and making us resort to dream books to find the answers we seek. However, the meaning cannot be expected to be exactly the same for everyone. Each person's life is different, and therefore the symbology for each and every one of us is unique and serves a different purpose in our growth and awareness.

Are you the type of person to seek out the meaning behind the symbols and do you then follow the paths they take you on? If the answer is yes, then you are— and continue to be—a very spiritually advanced soul. If you do not follow the paths the symbols will occur less and less.

Your higher state of consciousness needs growth just as the physical body needs food. If a muscle is not used over a period of time it atrophies or, in other words, it shrinks due to lack of use.

To stimulate higher consciousness activity, you should meditate daily for at least twenty minutes. There are many good books published on meditation. After a week you should notice a decisive difference in your sense of awareness to your surroundings. You should be able to gain new insight into the meaning of life, and feel joy in discovering abundant knowledge and the love that accompanies it. Begin your meditations and continue with them faithfully. Practice them with a sincere desire to grow spiritually, and you will be placed in contact with higher intelligences who will contact you during sleep.

I have been in communication with entities before I had any idea what was taking place. I thought everyone had, and was aware of such experiences. One night in June when I was 12 years old and living in Cleveland, Ohio, my father told me to go out and empty the trash. I remember going out the front door because the back door was blocked by a ladder. As I stepped outside, everything became misty. Suddenly I was aware that I wasn't in Cleveland anymore. (I can certainly sympathize with Dorothy from the Wizard of Oz!)

I still had the trash in my hands so I set the bag down. I saw what appeared to be a small circular metal craft. Now, I had just watched "The Day The Earth Stood Still" on TV a few days earlier so in my mind's eye I knew I must be dreaming, so

I just "played along" with the events at hand. I was curious so, of course, I went inside the craft. I heard someone coming and dream or not, this was a little spooky. I hid behind what looked like a computer, but in those days I had never heard of computers or seen one. My knowledge consisted of learning to clean and cook. We were old fashioned people. I heard a voice say, "You can't hide, we know you are here; we are not going to hurt you."

I came out and I saw two "men." They looked just like regular people to me. They sat me in a big chair. I guess I fell "asleep" in my dream because the next thing I remember is the ship being in a totally different place, because now there was a large lush green meadow surrounded by tropical vegetation. There were horses grazing peacefully when all of a sudden a herd of zebra came out of the forest and attacked the horses! These were not ordinary zebra as they had claws instead of hooves. When they attacked they ripped the horses' flesh and drove them off.

Then one of the men came back to the ship. He seemed perturbed that I had left my seat. I was horrified by what I had just seen. The man was not, however. Then he said to me, "Do not try to understand all that you see. Knowledge is gained through acceptance."

Well, for years, I thought many times about this experience. It was so vivid, I could remember it so well. I have a son now who is eleven years old and he talks constantly about becoming an archaeologist. Recently, I bought him a book about dinosaurs. I decided to browse through it when I came across a creature that according to the book was an ancestor of the zebra. It looked very much like the creature I had seen in my dream. It even had claws instead of hooves. I read the adjoining description. It claimed that these prehistoric zebra had claws used for digging and for defense!

Then it really hit me! Either I had an out of body experience, a close encounter, or I had a dream vision. I feel that someday it is possible that this animal will be discovered still living in South America, as well as I feel this is where the experience took place. Perhaps someday my son will become the archaeologist he dreams of beomg and discover this long-thought-to-be-extinct creature.

In the Bible, it constantly talks of the prophets and wise men and women of old talking with the "angels" in their dreams. Time and time again they are given both warnings and information. If the angel had not "appeared" to Joseph in a dream we might still be waiting for the teachings of Jesus.

We are told repeatedly that ETs cannot physically interfere with man's affairs. Ah! But they can contact us if we allow them to in our dreams. Visions and dreams have always had their place in the various religions of the world, lending credence to the fact that there is contact from higher intelligence.

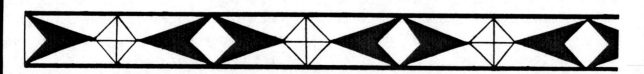

STRANGERS FROM ANOTHER WORLD

I met Dennis, an American Indian, at the annual gathering of a group presided over by Aileen Edwards. The UFO Contact Center International is a global support group for those individuals who have experienced abductions or contacts with other-worldly beings. One of the avenues of research the group does is reporting on the possible link between the Gods of the American Indian tribes and the reality of extraterrestrial and/or interdimensional beings. Dennis deals in this chapter with the various "life forms" taken for granted by his Red Brothers. Indeed, Indian tribes offer many strange legends about spook lights and bizarre forms of life from hairy giants to bobcats with the face of humans. The author of this article is a native American who has observed first hand that which his forefathers have passed on in their traditions.

I come from a country that is 7,000 to 10,000 feet above sea level, with ponderosa and high pines. It is known for what we call spook lights. They are usually red or blue. We have a lava flow that is undatable. Some archaeologists have tried to date it, but they can't figure out when it erupted. We have a couple of active volcano areas. There are a few areas which cannot be explored because of the terrain. The Indians have many legends about these areas.

When I was growing up, I remember seeing lights zip across the sky. These lights would not originate in the lava flow. They would originate somewhere else and then go to the lava flow. There have been archaeologists in the area. Most of them don't make it past midnight. Something scares them!

I took one of them out one night into an area which the Indians call "doshi-wee," meaning small dunies. The Ishiwee tribe is the one that's in that area. It's an unusual area because it's an active volcano. In the winter there is anywhere from two to eight feet of snow. Temperatures may drop to 39 below. Yet in this one area, there are plants which couldn't exist anywhere else because they would freeze.

This area is between Grants, New Mexico and Raymond, New Mexico. Azuni, New Mexico is the tribal center there. If you stand in the center of town and look south, a large, picturesque mountain would be to your left. When the sun comes up on the solstice, it comes up right over the top of the town, over the top of this mountain.

There are two rocks there through which the sun shines down to the middle of town. Legend has it that Coronado and some of his explorers stumbled into Azuni just at the solstice. Because the town was all cut sandstone, there was a lot of silica and silicates in it. So it looked like gold and they thought they had found the seven cities of Samola.

There have been a lot of occasions when unusual things have happened. Once, when I was about ten or eleven, we were camping out in the mountains, next to the volcanic crater. We spotted lights that night.

Three months later, during the latter part of August, we were having our manhood traditional ritual. What happens is you are taken out to an area blindfolded and left there. You are supposed to stay in that area for 24 to 48 hours, depending on how big of a wimp they think you are. A few don't make it. The first time I went out, I didn't make it. The canyon, just below me, lit up as bright as day. Being very young, I decided that running through the cactus at high speed and jumping barbed wire fences would be safer than sticking around. So I went screaming back to the village.

Later on, when I was about thirteen or fourteen, I decided to try it again. A similar thing happened, only this time, when I noticed the large lights, I went to explore and see what was going on. By the time I got to the area, there was nothing there. The lights had dimmed and gone away.

The tradition up there tells of different types of visitations. I grew up with people who believed that if there was a visitation, it was our government causing it. If we had a flying saucer in the area, it had a U.S. Air Force sticker on it. Later on, these people became very unsettled by things they had seen out there.

On December 18, 1967 we were having our traditional races. It was about eleven o'clock when a couple of red dots appeared over the horizon. They looked like they were sitting right on the mountain. Then within a few seconds they took off across the sky. On their way across they did a few tricks. They stopped right on the horizon of the other side, and then they went across the horizon and disappeared. Everyone went in for a prayer and meditation and decided to see what was going on.

There were reports of witch doctors who started their walk in New Mexico and all of a sudden showed up in Mexico, traveling two or three thousand miles in a couple of days. The witch doctor who did this was old when I was growing up and he's still around. I met him and I remember him from the time when I was two or three years old. He still walks through the desert, still makes his meditation runs and his medicine runs. He has some charms that are very unusual.

Even the Indians that I met in California had legends. I got into the Yeti/Bigfoot legends when I was in the Service. I found that the many tribes which were up on Mount Shasta all had a joint story. It was about a baby born from a sphere that had fallen from the sky. They were supposed to be stronger than normal and hairier than normal. They were supposed to have all kinds of abnormal characteristics. They could not speak as we do, yet they communicated among themselves.

I've had two experiences with American Yeti, and a couple of experiences with who knows what they were. I was where the lava flows, in a place call "The Hole." It's a natural insert in the ground, which was very unsettled because the lava flows had erupted around it. The "Hole" has a great geothermal potential. There are springs which bubble all year around. We measured the temperature for one year and there was less then a seven-degree variation from summer to winter.

The area is well traveled by Indians and wild game. The animals seem to congregate there, especially during a cold spell. The does will go there to have their young. It's a natural protection. They can defend it very easily, because there is only one way in, through a crack.

This crack is just wide enough so that a horse could walk through it. Once you are in there, you discover it is a maze of caves.

There have been two anthropologists from the Denver Museum out there. The first one made it until about 10:30. At that point, something came into the camp and drove us out. At first I said, "Don't get away from this fire. If you get away from this light, there are only two people who can protect you and neither one of them walk on earth." He didn't believe me, so he jumped up and went chasing it. My dog had been in there so many times that he quit barking at them. My horse started acting up. Ttwo minutes later the man was packing up and heading for his jeep.

These creatures are not Bigfoot. Their height is about 3'11", maybe four feet. I've never seen them during the day. I know that they walk on two legs. They are also ambidextrous, since they open jars. They just love dill pickles. I even baited a trap with dill pickles. They managed to get the pickles without setting off the trip wires.

I thought I was very skilled at photographing animals at night. I set up a trap with four cameras pointed at this dill pickle jar. I even opened the jar for them, so they could smell it. They still got the dill pickles without tripping the trap so they must have some intelligence.

One moonlit night I did get a picture of an adult female. She must have had more than average curiosity because she got between me and the moon and I silhouetted her. At first I thought it was a bear, because it was stumbling through the bushes around the hot well where I was camping. I was just wondering what was between me and that hot well when she walked into the moonlight.

She looked like a female of about fourteen years of age (our size). You could tell that she had breasts. One thing I could never figure out is that they don't look like they have a neck. I don't know if it's because of the hair or what.

There are a lot of berries and strawberries in this area. They've got wild strawberries up there as big as your thumb. That's what brought me there. Also there are very few bears. This is very unusual because the country up there is known for its large black and brown bears. The deer and other game are more

There is a growing feeling that the American Indian may eventually lead many of the worthy to a safe new world.

plentiful in that area, probably because it's impossible to get a vehicle in there. There are a lot of unexplainable trails in there. A lot of domestic animals don't like going back in there. There are some birds in there which I have never seen anywhere else.

I told a wildlife biologist about them and he said that they only exist here in this area. I told him I could show him where they exist at 9,000 feet. I also told him that hawks fly in groups of five and six, and that there were fix or six different species in that area. He told me that hawks don't fly in community type situations.

The most unusual thing that I've seen there is a Bobcat with no hair on the face. This put the young lady I was with in the hospital in a state of shock. We were horseback riding and we got stranded out there. We ended up in the place called the "hole" because it was starting to get cold that night. I really thought it was a Bobcat, when I saw it running off. She, however, described it as a person's face on a bobcat's body.

It gave her quite a shock so I took her back to the car. Just as I sat down something jumped on the hood of the car. It turned around and looked at us and sure enough, it was this cat. I instantly went into shock. I locked all the doors and sat there, staring at it for quite a while.

A friend of mine later explained that White Sands is within 150 miles of the area. With the nuclear testing that goes on in the area, there is the possibility of a nuclear freak. I couldn't accept that explanation because I've seen what radiation does to animals. It could cause amorphism, but this gross an amorphism I couldn't swear. I went back to the reservation and spoke with someone who I thought would know. I found Shuntola, the medicine man up in the mountains, as he was coming back from Mexico. All I had to do was describe what I thought I had seen and he told me where I was when I saw it. He told me that I should not go there. He called it "questions that could not be answered or answers that have no questions." It is difficult to translate what he said because he speaks an ancient Zuni language which is more Zuni than Spanish. Today Zuni is more Spanish than Zuni. He also told me that I should buy forty feathers and thank the gods that I had made it out of there.

I went back to the same area about two weeks later to make sure I wasn't going nuts. Recently, I returned to the "hole" and stayed for two days. I was visited in a way that was different from before. They didn't bother me at all, or tear up my camp, or anything. I could hear them moving around in the bushes. I went swimming in the steam and then came back to my camp but it was undisturbed. But I found a turquoise turtle sitting in my camp. Before that I used to find tools missing.

I took some pots from the area to the Denver Museum. While I was messing around, I found the bones of a Spanish Conquistador who had passed away up there.

Though I have spent much time in the area, the place always intrigues me because of its many unanswered questions.

THE KACHINAS—
REPRESENTATIVES OF
THE GODS

If you are traveling in the western United States and should happen to visit a souvenir shop, you will see these strange looking dolls for sale which, if you didn't know better, you would think represented beings from outer space. Well, actually the author of this chapter, Clair Millet, known also as Day-Ga-Chee — the Man With Red Whiskers, says these dolls, known as "Kachinas" may well be symbolic of the star people who traveled down and visited with the early Indian settlers and taught spiritual and meditation practices. There is a general belief among the tribes that the Kachinas are soon to return as our planet enters a new age. (This article first appeared in the now defunct New Atlantean Journal.)

The word "Kachina" reminds most white people only of dolls, elegantly carved and ornamented and sold in tourist shops or collected in museums. . . . What they think of as "Kachinas" are really no more than toys, made originally to teach the young to recognize the various Kachinas appearing in the dances that mark important events in the Hopi calendar. It is actually very difficult to define what a Kachina is, because the same word applies simultaneously to the dancer impersonating a certain spirit and to the spirit itself, as well as to the person, animal, or plant that the spirit infuses. For the Hopi, everything in nature has a spiritual dimension, a spirit being who controls that person or animal or plant, and acts as a messenger to the gods when the Pueblo people wish to send a message.

These spirits are believed to live on the peaks of the San Francisco mountains from mid-July until late December or early January, when they descend to visit the Pueblo tribes. The Hopi calendar begins with this descent and the Kachina ceremonies are the most elaborate of the dances—which are performed to invoke their air. POWAMU, or the Bean Dance, takes place in February and celebrates the continued appearance of green plants during winter. At this time the young men are initiated into the tribe. POWAMU prepares for spring and sets things in order. From this point on, the Kachinas dance weekly in the plaza, or if it is too cold, in the Kiva. This close association of the spirits and the Hopi continues until the NIMAN KACHINA, or Home Dance. About ten days after the summer solstice, the tribe prepares for the departure of these spirits, and in this final ceremony the Indians present the Kachinas with their prayers for the months until the next POWAMU, with reminders of things they will need, such as water and food.

During a Kachina ceremony, the dancers feel that they have lost their individual identities and become the deities they represent. The dances they perform help accomplish this infusion and allow the people a chance to communicate with the spirits. There are two main styles or types of Kachina dance, often referred to by the names of the tribes performing them in the purest fashion, the Hopi type and the Rio Grande. The Hopi Kachina dancers sing as they dance. They enter the Plaza and line up along one side of the square and sing the first verse relevant to that ceremony. . . .

Today a steady erosion of meaning plagues the ceremonies, as fewer and fewer young men take an active interest in the full meaning of the dance and the mythology that lies behind it. The ranks of the priesthood are only renewed by the initiation of new priests (calling for an especially elaborate version of dances that year) once in about four years. In the meantime, dances are simpler and have now become a combination of social event for the Indians and a tourist attraction.

There are Kachina masks called "Ancients" which have been passed on from tribes who have vanished to their kindred, who revere them but cannot tell exactly what they mean. Sadly, more and more of the traditional masks are becoming "ancients" in this sense.

Told for the first time, the Apache story of the origin of Camelback, Four Peaks, Hole in the Rock, and the Superstition Mountains of Arizona.

I can't swear this story is true, but I heard it from a dying woman, the guardian of her people's legends. In telling this tale, I am making good my pledge to her that night, to keep the story alive when she has gone. (Note: The New Atlantean Journal also has made similar pledges to many, who have now gone Home, not to let their words and deeds lie covered by the ashes of unspoken Time.)

Because I am deeply interested in Indian lore and traditions, I have spent many years studying and painting their ceremonial dances. I have become friends with many of them. It was through one such friendship with an Apache medicine man that I was invited to the very impressive CHANGING WOMAN CEREMONIAL (Apache Crown Dance) for his daughter. Few white men are invited to these very personal, sacred ceremonies. I took it as a high compliment when I was asked to come. I recall the magic that drew around us even as we arrived at the ceremonial site in the mountains northeast of Phoenix. It was raining steadily and rivulets of water ran down the tracks in the dirt road ahead of us. "Looks like bad weather for the dances," I observed to an old medicine man. He shrugged and replied, "No. I made the medicine to move the storm away until we're through." The rain soon turned to a light drizzle, then stopped. Not until the fourth day just as we drove away from the meeting place did the rain

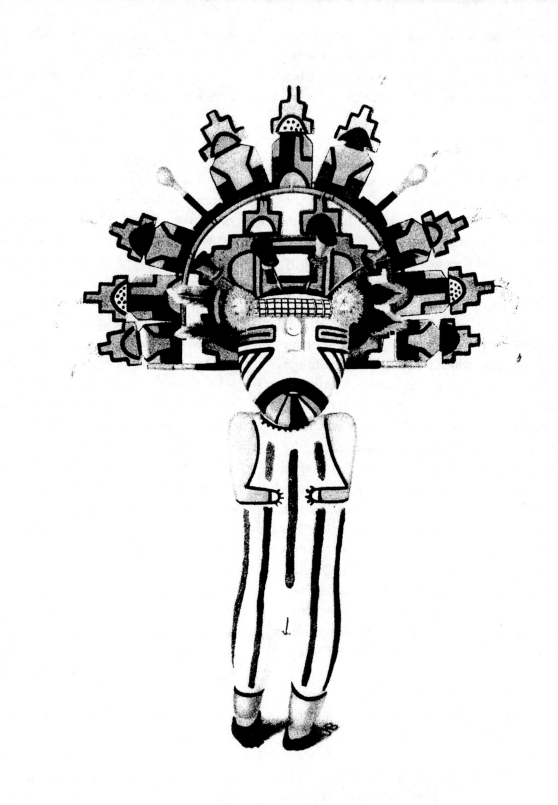

Hopi Kachina spirit.

clouds come back again. My daughter and I spent four days with the San Carlos Apaches and their guests from the Mescallero Apache tribe. I lent a hand in the cooking, corn grinding and wood gathering, as my daughter did. . . .

There was a rustling of leaves, a snapping of twigs, the crunch of feet and the whisper of cloth brushing the undergrowth as two figures came toward us. As they entered the ring of light diffused by my fire, I recognized an elderly white-haired Apache woman I had ground corn for, and her granddaughter. . . Without preamble, the Apache grandmother leaned forward and said in a high-pitched voice, "You asked about stories. I will give you one because I like you and trust you. I will die very soon and I do not want my story to go to my grave with me." She asked me to pledge that I would preserve the story. . . I swore to do so, and she slowly began the tale of the TUAR-TUMS, the little Indians who live down in the "Big Valley" (The Salt River Valley or "Valley of the Sun") and the JIAN-DU-PIDS, the giants who invaded their land, stole their water, ruined their fields, drove them underground and were finally seared into the earth by the Great Father, the Sun.

"Long, long ago, long before the people you call Ho-Ho-Kam came here and dug the first irrigation canals, a little tiny people lived in the Big Valley. They were like so (holding up a hand), about three feet high. Good farmers, using water from the Salt River to grow fine crops and raise fat animals. They were very happy, singing and chanting as they worked, until the JIAN-DU-PIDS came."

She described the coming of enormous Indians, apparently as big as Paul Bunyon, who used a tree for a toothpick. They came, dragging with them massive sleds containing all their wealth. Their vast horde of gold weighed down a mountainous camel (she called it a Bay-ze-lea). They also had with them a huge reddish-brown hunting dog whose head stood as high as the knees of his masters. It swept on ahead, killing the TUAR-TUMS and their animals and ruining their fields. The giants came from the Northeast, headed for their old home in the South, led by Evil-kin, a massive, hulking man who struck fear to the hearts of all who saw him. When they reached the Roosevelt Lake area, they decided they could go no farther by land, that they must build a ship to carry them Southwest to their home beyond the Gulf of Baja. But where could they find enough water in the parched desert to float such a tremendous ship?

The tiny TUAR-TUMS lived in the Big Valley using the water from the river to supply their needs—until the giants came into the valley and diverted all the rivers, creeks and streams, destroying the dams and canals. In trying to do this, they destroyed much of the civilization the TUAR-TUMS had built up. Many were killed, their farms and homes ruined.

For a time, the JIAN-DU-PIDS returned to the North to bring in more gold and supplies, but the TUAR-TUMS knew they would come again. To save their lives, the little people decided to build everything underground — their homes, their farms, even divert the rivers into the Under Valley. Since there were large honey-combed caverns already in existence, this was not an impossible task. To the East, the Four Peaks each held a TUAR-TUM sentry facing one of the four points of the compass. The lookouts signaled with polished copper shields to a central watchkeeper in the Valley to warn of the return of the Enemy.

KASSKARA – THE LOST PARADISE

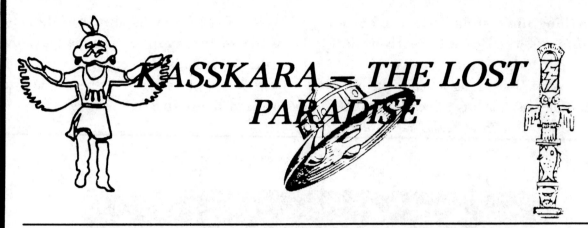

Lost cities and hidden cultures have always been intriguing. Hans Peterson though he is a Danish researcher fully realizes that fact as he analyses the work of Professor Blumrich in regard to Kasskara, the Lost Paradise, and the American Indian belief in other worlds and the ending of an age. Peterson's influence is the late contactee, George Adamski whose encounters with beings from other planets were the subject of several books in the 1950s and 1960s. He believes that the Indians remain in communication with more advanced beings because of their own purity and feelings toward the living Earth.

The book *Kasskara and the Seven Worlds* is so filled with important details that I have decided to give a summary of its general lines. It contains so many "technical" as well as cosmic details that anybody who has read the works of George Adamski, UFO contactee, should not miss this book.

All the information given in this article originates from the traditions of the Hopi and from the author of Kasskara, Josef F. Blumrich, a retired NASA engineer. As we are dealing with the entire Indian civilization, both from North, Central and South American continents, originating from the two lost worlds of Lemuria and Atlantis, we shall primarily hear of these areas whereas Europe, the Middle East and Africa only are mentioned in passing, and Asia is more or less left out. The "beginning of life" is a natural starting point for the population of that part

of the world we are to hear about. Through their traditions the Hopi are acquainted with that period of time, and their knowledge is exact enough to be believed. Of course, the planet Earth also existed before the period we shall hear about, but from that period there is nothing but darkness — yet. Maybe that period of time will also be unveiled some day.

The Hopi know of the existence of 4 worlds out of the 7 worlds we are to go through before the planet Earth gets a new and higher status. We are now in the middle of our time, but soon also this world will disappear and the fifth world will be born.

No one remembers any details from the first world; they know it was destroyed by fire; the surviving part of the populations escaped to the second world.

Geographically the second world was situated where the present two American continents are placed. When it disappeared through a semi-tipping of the Earth, it was covered by an ocean. Simultaneously, the third world emerged from the sea, and thus Kasskara (Lemuria) and Taláwaitzchqua (Atlantis) came into existence. At that time Europe, the Middle East and Africa are known to exist; North and South America were under sea-level. Nothing is mentioned about the Asian continent.

In order to be able to understand some of the immense activities of nature resulting in destruction of some continents and birth (rebirth) of others, we must understand that our world — the crust of Earth on which we are living — is divided into so-called continental plates of a thickness from 40 to 60 km. In order to see how very little that is in comparison to the Earth itself, we can compare the Earth with a globe the diameter of 30 cm. What corresponds to our crust of earth will then be about 2.5 mm. thick.

These plates are floating and shifting, thereby causing earth trembling, volcanic eruptions and the worldwide cataclysms where old worlds disappear under sea-level through a technique of tipping while others emerge. These cataclysms do not happen at random but are proportional to the pattern of life appearing on the continental plates. To this fact the philosophy of the Hopi has the following comments:

Corruption, immorality, and wars always provoke destructive catastrophes, and humanity and nature always reach this very critical point simultaneously.

In order to have a better understanding of the activities of the plates, I shall give you their names:

The Australian plate
The Pacific plate
The North American plate
The Nazca plate
The South American plate
The African plate

In this connection I can mention that where the Pacific and the North American plates are meeting, and where the Pacific, the Australian and the Eurasian plates are meeting, or rather colliding, big catastrophes in Los Angeles and Tokyo, respectively, can be expected before long.

TRADITION OF THE HOPI

The traditions of the Hopi take their beginning in the third world after having arrived there over an extremely long period from the first and via the second world. This third world is recalled by the Hopi through their traditions. As corruption, immorality and wars had perverted Nature, this world also disappeared, and the fourth world — our world — emerged from the waves and divided the big ocean into the Atlantic Ocean and the Pacific Ocean. This happened 80,000 years before everybody from Lemuria had reached the American continent. Only a few from Atlantis survived, however, and those who did escape came to Europe, the Middle East and Africa. After a very long period some of them started a new development which resulted in the area we today know as Egypt.

In the third world they had reached a stage of development similar to our present stage; well, actually even further, for beyond a technical society with planes, satellites and space flights to other planets, they also had flying saucers.

In Atlantis they had constructed these advanced spaceships and flew them themselves. The Lemurians, however, had them made on other planets, and they were flown by space people, all for the benefit of the population of Lemuria. A physical evidence of flying in earlier times — although not that far back in history — is found in the Piri Reis map. But, in fact, there are maps showing all parts of the world, all of which would have been possible only by measurements from the air, and they all date at least 8,000 years back in time.

The philosophy of the Hopi tells us that space people have been present here on Earth at all times until some time not long ago when they left Earth, which we shall hear about later on. The space people have many different names through the ages, but in the history of the Hopi they are called Kachinas. In Mexico, they are called Viracochaes, and today we most frequently come across two names. Here I will only use the name Kachinas — a Kachina — a spaceman from another planet. In the Hopi language Kachina means "High, Esteemed Wiseman in Constant Development." The world they came from had 12 planets and they used magnetic power for flying — also in our atmosphere. There were three types of Kachinas:

1.   The ordinary Kachinas — whom we nowadays could compare with the biblical angels. They were the working space people.
2.   The next group were the higher ranging Kachinas. They were the leaders, and today we could compare them with the biblical archangels. There were the philosophical teachers, among others, teaching about continuation of life.
3.   Finally there were the supreme beings who watched that the cosmic laws were observed and who gave warnings in case of an offense.

Kasskara — Lemuria — was the size of Asia today and covered 40-50 degrees of longitude and 60-90 degrees of latitude with about 20 degrees north of the Equator and at least 30 degrees south of Equator. Hawaii is a remnant of Lemuria and is expected to have belonged to the northern area. To the south the Easter Island is a remnant of Lemuria. This island is expected to have belonged to the most southern area.

In Lemuria all power and energy was generated from the Sun, and it could be done everywhere. No wires were needed, but today nobody knows how they did it. Furthermore they had a device with a crystal. In those days they did not have to chisel a stone for days in order to split it. They only had to hold the device in such a way that the Sun was reflected in the crystal, and any stone was split in no time.

THE GREAT CRYSTAL

All sounds from the many thousand years Kasskara existed were stored in a crystal, and this crystal is now to be found in a cave in South America, but nobody knows where.

At that time they were also able to raise huge blocks of rock by stretching out their arms and hands, and they did not even have to touch them. Today we not even have to touch them. Today we are surprised and do not understand how they could build these huge cities, the ruins of which we are finding nowadays. But it is quite simple. The greatest power of the human body is concentrated in the fingers from where an enormous power is radiating, but much power can also be absorbed.

They also worked with quicksilver, both solid and fluid, but today nobody remembers how. It had something to do with heat and balance.

The human beings were highly developed at that time, but all their knowledge was lost, and they had to start afresh. In comparison to what they mastered then, we can say that we today are living in the age of darkness — that little do we know.

In the ancient cities, both in the third world and in the beginnings of our fourth world, all circular buildings were symbolizing the feminine, and all square buildings the masculine. Of great importance were the keyhole forms and the T-forms as they were symbolizing the plan of the Creator.

The Hopi know that our voices and thoughts up through all the worlds remain imprinted in the atmosphere, and that they cannot be destroyed — they remain there forever. The Hopi also know that the human beings in Kasskara had been reincarnated from previous worlds.

Many Hopi became of high cosmic rank, and they were allowed to fly together with the Kachinas in their spaceships.

However, Atlantis had a very bad influence on parts of the Lemurian people, even from the ruling classes and the scientific community, and finally they once more started a space research program long before they were spiritually developed to do so.

Atlantis was a rather small territory but highly influential like England in its palmy days. Geographically, it was situated between our present Central America and Africa, roughly speaking, with its center at our present Sargasso Sea. Like all others at that time they had contact with and worked with the Kachinas, but as just mentioned, they went their own way and constructed flying saucers, started a space research program, developed dreadful weapons and conquered parts of or the whole of Europe, the Middle East and Africa.

In the last phase Atlantis had a great influence on Lemuria where many people joined them and worked together with the enemy hoping for profit. Finally, Atlantis started a war with terrible magnetic weapons against Lemuria. The Lemurians knew of these weapons and were able to protect themselves against them, but suddenly the cataclysm occurred. At that time the Kachinas left Atlantis.

Atlantis soon disappeared below sea-level. However, 8,000 years passed before all Lemuria had disappeared below sea-level. As a possible remnant from Atlantis you can meet the most remarkable traditions today in France, England and Ireland; and the origin of the Basque language is still unknown. Reference is also made to burial places and cromlechs from the Megalithic age which are older than the buildings of the Middle East. They form a belt along the European coasts from southern Spain to southern Sweden plus Ireland, Malta and the western parts of England. None of these cromlechs are situated more than 145 km. from the sea.

Of course, the Kachinas knew that the cataclysm would come. Since Lemuria as a whole nation had made no violation of the cosmic laws and had always cooperated, the Kachinas helped the Lemurian people with the evacuation to the islands which had emerged from the sea to the far east. Favored by a slow destruction they succeeded in reaching a new country over a period of 8,000 years. This new country they named Táotoóma, the present North and South America.

Firstly, the tribes who were to prepare the new world were evacuated, and it is indeed interesting to see how they were chosen. The Kachinas made the choice. The first tribes were:

The fire tribe — which were to undertake the supply of energy.

The snake tribe — which supplied the architects who were to build houses and roads.

The spider tribe — which was to undertake the communication system, telephone and telegraph, etc.

The bow tribe — which was to undertake history and the press.

The eagle tribe — which was to undertake the problems regarding flight, satellites, and preparation for space travel.

The water tribe — which was to supply the engineers for the building of the water supply and the building of dams, etc.

The lizard tribe — which was to prepare for the arrival of the border of society, such as the nervously ill and the homosexuals.

The first group of experts and their families were evacuated by flying saucers. The next group was evacuated by ordinary aeroplanes when the time had come. The third and last of the groups were evacuated by ship. The Kachinas undertook the evacuation of the first two groups — the third group, however, had to make the journey on their own. However, each tribe was given a Kachina to lead the way and to give advice which the tribes could take or leave.

It took thousands of years before the last of the people had arrived, partly because of the tremendous amount of water, and because it was necessary to sail from island to island. Often the tribes settled on an island for generations until they were given a sign by the Kachinas to pack and carry on.

Gradually, as the evacuated tribes arrived in the new world, they were told where to settle by the Kachinas. They were well aware that everything had been prepared for their arrival, so the Kachinas took it for granted that the tribes followed the orders they were given.

The first group, which had arrived by flying saucers, settled in the new island empire on the banks of a lagoon, and here they built the city of Táotoóma — or Tiahuanaco, as we know it today. The city at its height was the same size as Los Angeles today, and had a huge harbor with enormous docking areas. In order to grow crops it was necessary to build terraces in the soil somewhat above sea-level as the flat soil still contained a great deal of salt — too much to produce any crops. As the land emerged, more terraces were built, under the others. This explains why we today still can find terraces at the

Symbol of Kasskara — Lost Paradise.

height of 5,000 meters. On the Illimani mountain in the Andes these terraces disappear under a glacier at the height of 5,500 meters. As the land rose, the lagoon was turned into a lake and thus creating the great Titicaca lake.

The country gradually became more and more expanded with towns, roads, etc. and the population became more and more scattered all over the country. Tunnels were built, and an underground tunnel system is supposed to exist under the whole of the South American continent. Recently an article was published stating that a tunnel system of more than 100 km. in length exists in Peru. It begins near Otuzco, not far from the old Inca road, and ends under sea-level close to the beach and not far from the island of Guanale, position: 8 degrees 35 mins. south. But an uncountable number of tunnels and caves are supposed to exist, and in many of them the most beautiful drawings, painted in wonderful colors, have been discovered. They have been found in the provinces of Zapotekas, Cuertlavaca and Tequiztepec.

All the buildings were built out of stone — often of enormous dimensions, and when looking at them today, one gets the impression that they were able to cut this stone as one cuts into cheese. Looking at the transcriptions of the Hopi, it is quite clear that they were able to do this. They also mastered a technique which enabled them to transport and lift these often very heavy blocks of stone without hindrance. These techniques, softening the stone and transporting and lifting such great burdens, we do not have any knowledge of today. Though these theories are being researched, the mystery remains unsolved. From the areas around Táotoóma — now Tiahuanaco — it is said white men with beards lived on an island on the Titicaca lake, and that they could cure the sick and make the blind see just by touching them. In Ecuador there lived men who were three times the size of the natives, and each of them ate more than 50 times as much as a native.

MYSTERIOUS FINDINGS

In 1550, bones were found in Lima, Peru, of human beings that were even bigger. Peter Acorta reported that he had seen the skeleton of a man where each tooth was bigger than a clenched fist, and the rest of the body was in proportion to this. In all the legends reports are made about flying machines, and among others Dr. Franco de Avila reported about these technical marvels in 1620.

A legend states that five large eggs landed on Condorcoto mountain in South America, and at the same time a storm raged such as never seen before. Out of the eggs stepped five falcons (persons in space suits), and when they had finished taking off their plumage they started at once to perform miracles. On the whole the Kachinas had whitish skin, had light hair and wore a beard. They had the highest thinkable morale, they were mighty, and they could in an instant change the surroundings into mountains, mountains into valleys, and make water run directly from a rock. Again and again it is said that they could fly, and it is also said that they disappeared under sea-level without reappearing. They spoke kindly to the natives and encouraged them to be good to each other, love one another and to be kind. They cured the sick simply by touching them, and they made many brilliant regulations for the ruling of the country. They taught natives how to use the plants for food as well as for curing people. They also taught them about the animals and how to treat them. The philosophy of the Kachinas which the Hopi fully obeyed (and still do) is realizing that everything stands in connection with each other. Being the highest intelligence on Earth, man has been pointed out to be the leader for his fellow creatures in nature, but he is not allowed just to take and use what he wants. On the contrary, he must ask permission to take these things as a gift. Man has permission to take from nature, but he must be aware that he is taking from his own substance — from his and his children's inheritance. With a respect of this kind for creation, care for the world and the gifts of nature, nature becomes natural.

By looking at the world as a living organism instead of a big confusion of different things it is easy to understand that every interference in an area automatically has an influence on many other areas. This shows how much wisdom there is in this attitude instead of the mechanical way of thinking we know of today, which has ruled out mental thinking for a long time. By cosmic thinking we gain an aversion to war and the murdering of people, and it makes it clear that there is a difference whether you kill another intelligent human form of in our society or you do not because the human being is the expression of the Creator for the highest intelligence. In the first case you break the laws of our planet; in the second case you go directly against the Creator.

There is nothing worse than killing another human being — nothing.

The Kachinas lived long and could be very old. In Venezuela there was a Kachina who reached the age of 1400 years, and in Bogota there was one who reached 2000 years.

After about 10,000 years in Tiahuanaco, groups again started to depart from the cosmic rules, and the town was completely left in ruins by a natural catastrophe. This happened about 70,000 years ago. Since the legends say that Tiahuanaco was built on top of a town which had been turned upside down, it is not possible for us to say how old the new city is — anyway, everybody says it has always been there.

GREAT CATASTROPHE

At the time of this great catastrophe the emigration to other areas in South America had already started for some time, but the catastrophe caused massive groups of the population to move in all directions. We shall now follow those who headed North. With help from the Kachinas as pathfinders and protectors they fought their way through the great jungle covering most of the continent. During the day the Kachinas were in front, behind and on both sides of the tribe, and during the night they hovered over the jungle and lit up the entire area where the tribe had settled for the night, keeping the wild animals at a distance.

Soon all the important tribes were on the move, and we can imagine a whole continent on the move. During these gigantic migrations the leaders of the cosmic-minded tribes decided to meet in a certain place and to have a new attempt at living in accordance with cosmic laws.

The Kachinas led all the involved tribes toward Central America where they built a big city — at that time the biggest north of the Equator. For the first time the building of the city was done without the aid of the Kachinas but by using their know-how. The town was named Palàtquapi — known in our day as Palenque. The tribes who did not wish to participate in this new society sank lower and lower mentally, and they never rose again. One can deduct from this that all the Indians on the American continent from the north down to Tierra del Fuego originally came from Palenque — Palàtquapi. Palàtquapi was known as the red city, and aside from being big it was very beautiful and important. The biggest and most important building in the city was a large four-story building which was used for education.

On the ground floor the students learned about the history of all tribes. On the second floor the students learned about the purpose of life. They learned all about nature and the plants and animals. They learned how the flowers grow, where the insects, the birds and the other animals come from and about everything that lives in the sea. How everything is born and develops, and telepathy was used to help understand all this. The chemical compounds were also learned. We are dependent on these in order to live. The body is composed of minerals that come from the earth. If we do not follow the cosmic rules and maltreat the Earth, not only shall we suffer mentally but also physically. All illness that is inflicted on man is the fault of man himself. Along with these studies the students learned how to grow food.

RESPECT FOR LIFE

In this way human beings with great respect for life were created. They were taught that it was the cosmic rules that they were to follow when they used plants and animals for food or materials for building of homes. Of course, they were allowed to do this but they had to ask permission to receive what they were to use, as a gift. Even today any educated Hopi prays and gives thanks for everything that he receives from nature. It is very important to do this.

One the third floor those pupils went who had been through the other two floors. Their age at this stage was between 12 and 20. So, before they came to the third floor they had learned all about the various people, their opinions and thoughts, and they were now old enough to have made some observations and had experiences. Now was the time to learn how the human body and soul stood in connection with the Creator.

Firstly, they dealt with the head. The Creator has given us a wonderful instrument to think with — the brain. In our brain our thoughts and decisions work in accordance with the physical part of the human nature. And they were taught about the structure of the soul, the Creator's influence on the human race and on everything that lives in the Cosmos. He who lives with these thoughts has no need to worry about language barriers; he can communicate with all the plants and animals, with every creation in the entire world. Apart from this they were to learn about the voice.

The sound waves we make when talking are not only restricted to those with whom we are speaking, but they fill the whole Cosmos. Therefore they must be harmonious. If they are, well, one praises the Creator. Everything we say is recorded. Everything a human being says in a whole lifetime does not exceed the size of a pinhead. All the voices, everything that has been said in the third world, is kept safe, as we said before, in a crystal inside a cave in South America.

Last of all the most important part of the education was all about the heart. In the heart the opinions of other people are made, and here we also find the understanding and pity which is necessary. The other important side of our heart activity is its connection with our blood which keeps our body alive. And because our blood is so important, man must never experiment with it. To a certain degree man has the same power as the Creator, but the Creator has the knowledge of secrets which man should have no knowledge about, and this ought to be taken seriously. In your world you have now gone so far as to experiment with artificial life — some day maybe human beings. This is what we Hopi call experimenting with blood, and it is not wise to do this.

FOURTH FLOOR

And finally we come to the fourth floor. Here the pupils were taught about the Universe which surrounds us and about the Creation and the divine power which is the ruler of all things. The pupils were taught all the details of our solar system — and not only the visible part of the system, but also its laws. They also learned that a universal plan of creation exists, a plan which man must follow. If man does not live in accordance with this plan, he is no longer considered a divine creature and has to be punished. The commandant of the Creator is very simple, but at the same time difficult to live up to: "All that hurts a human being and all that is destroying its peace is inconsistent with the Creator's commandment." According to this rule, the worst crime given is to kill another person.

The instruction was given by the Kachinas, and they reported back to their home planets about the progress of the pupils. Once in a while they disappeared with lightening speed to visit their relatives at home. The Kachinas also made the decision who were going to be pupils in the big school because they were the only ones who knew the children before they were born. That was also the reason why the Kachinas were able to decide whether the pupils could advance from one floor to the next one. Many pupils did not succeed in getting further than to the first, the second or at best the third floor, and very few advanced to the last floor.

The physical and spiritual life of those who "graduated" was in complete harmony with the divine Creator, and they were now allowed to be called "great, holy men." One of these men has said that it is possible to see from our physical world into the spiritual world. The borderline between the physical and the spiritual area is very diffuse, and anyone who can use his telepathic ability is able to go from one area into the other just as he wishes. He also said that if the telepathic ability is used, it is possible to look at the opposite side of the Earth by means of a bowl of water and the light of the Moon.

The few people who reached the top floor at the school in Palátquapi were rewarded by the Kachinas — they should not die. At a certain time they could leave the Earth alive and did not have to die. Previously this also was seen in Táotoóma. Earth-people really left Earth from Táotoóma in their physical bodies and were taken to the planets from where the Kachinas came, and they never returned to Earth.

Through centuries people in Palátquapi remained faithful to the cosmic belief — Harmony was everywhere. But then a few again started to break the cosmic laws which resulted in others doing the same, and soon many again deviated from the right course. The result was that the diverging tribes left Palátquapi and settled somewhere else on the Yuccatan, and they built among other things the big pyramids at Tikal and Chichen Itza. Finally only a few "cosmic-minded" people were left in Palátquapi.

Then after a while the emigrated tribes attacked the cosmic-minded people who had remained in Palátquapi. Even though they succeeded in defending themselves, they decided to leave the territory. This happened in deep secrecy, and without anyone getting caught. Afterwards the town was destroyed by an earthquake.

When all this happened the Kachinas left Earth physically, and they have not been seen ever since even if they, up to our time, have helped and still do help in other ways. The war which took place on Yuccatan was fought with advanced magnetic weapons.

Up through the ages the tribes spread further. As mentioned before, these Indians originated from Táotoóma, and later from Palátquapi. Now they populate the American continent from the Arctic Ocean to the North to Tierra del Fuego to the South, together with an alien tribe which immigrated via the Bering Strait after the Ice Age. And also together with the white colonists — their former enemies from Atlantis — who now, back on their feet again, returned to conquer what they were prevented from conquering in earlier times. So the population on the American continent today is a crossbreed of the old one from Lemuria and the aliens from Atlantis. The population of the Middle East also originates from Atlantis. The people from Atlantis are militant, corrupt and selfish; the Lemurians are gentle, mild and modest — in other words, cosmic.

Many tribes did not fulfill the big new migration which the Gods had commanded should take place from South to North and from West to East and back again. They settled in places they liked, and that's the reason why there is such an enormous dispersal. During these immense migrations the people always left marks to tell that they had been in this place so that the tribes to follow were able to study their movements so far. In a certain area at Nazca in the Andes people left their tribe-symbol on the surface of the Earth. Thus later passing tribes as well as the Gods were able to see who had been at this point of intersection, and which way they had taken when they left the place [partly my own theory — (HC)]. To illustrate the great dispersal of the tribes it can be mentioned that in the Amazon district alone 20 different languages are known, and more than 700 dialects are supposed to exist.

ORDER OF THE GODS

The orders of the Gods said that the big migration was to be carried through by all tribes, and afterwards they were allowed to settle down permanently. The people who finished their migration first settled and built a city which they called Oraibi, and called themselves Hopi. All the people who came later in order to become members of this permanent society had to prove that they had not broken the cosmic laws, and that they essentially were able to conduce to both the material and spiritual existence of this new society. If they were not able to do this, they were sent away and had to find another place to settle. Anybody who was admitted to the new society was automatically called a Hopi. One of the tribes which was turned away was the Aása tribe. Afterwards it emigrated to Mexico and became the Aztecs.

At times of lack of food the Kachinas helped the starving people by telling and showing them how to shake a bowl of grain and pick up the few grains which first fell to the ground. These grains were to be put into a basket or a bowl and placed in a dark room in the house. Every time they went to the bowl it had mysteriously been filled with food, and in this way they were able to get what they needed to survive.

When you met the Kachinas and asked them where they came from, they would answer, "The Universe is my home." And often, when such a contact was made and you turned to ask for more, they had disappeared. [Please notice that the behavior of the space-people at that time was exactly the same as today (HC)]. The space-people also stated that they did not eat our kind of food but fed themselves by the spirit that existed in the food. They said it this way: "It is just like nourishing from water that comes from a snowflake when it thaws."

The solar system, from which they came, consists of twelve planets. However, our scientists do not yet know it, and it will not be discovered until the 7th world is coming to its end. At that time the Earth will be admitted to a community of solar systems.

The Hopi continue: "Naturally the scientists and experts of today will oppose and try to correct most of what we tell here, just the way they always do, because they do not understand anything. We are people of a spiritual outlook, and if you want to study us, our history and our philosophy, you must learn to understand us. Otherwise, you will not be able to understand our history."

When people formerly made wars or in some other way broke the cosmic laws, the Kachinas said, "This is the world of the human being, and what he is doing here must be his own responsibility. So he can do whatever he wants without any interference from our side."

Our previous worlds were destroyed because we broke the cosmic laws. As it may be difficult to understand, we can compare it with the big nations all over the world today. They all want power and their part of the cake, and they use all means to get it. This leads to an offence against the cosmic laws in all fields.

When the punishment for corruption, immorality and warfare very shortly will overtake the people in our world, it will just be a recurrence of what has happened before in the three previous worlds. A terrible war will come where the atomic weapons will not be the worst. New advanced magnetic weapons will be used, weapons that are still in the course of preparation, or even finished — just as it happened in Lemuria, Atlantis and at Palátquapi. The Hopi "do not know how these weapons work, but something is sent out from a transmitter, and it is spread like radio waves and penetrates everything. There is no protection against this in our world."

When the Kachinas left the Earth on Yuccatan they must have realized that there was nothing more for them to do here on Earth. We did not want to listen to them — we could manage by ourselves. They made a last attempt to save their "white children" when they gave their instructions to the big school in Palátquapi. But when wars, in spite of this, broke out there was no getting round it. They had to realize that they could not save the population on the Earth.

An experiment which had covered a very long period [perhaps 200,000 years (HC)] had come to an end, and now they had no other choice but to return to their home planets.

However, the Hopi keep a lot of knowledge and wisdom from the last activities of the Kachinas here on Earth. The teachings of the Kachinas have been lost to the world as such, and it was not until George Adamski again removed the veil that we were able to take up the thread and put two and two together! Where would we be without him? [The remark about Adamski is mine (HC)] The teaching covered all the best human qualities, and if you do not constantly cultivate and observe it, it will die. The objects of Atlantis were easier to attain and more attractive to us, and so they survived and inspire our whole world today.

The tragedy of the Kachinas — the space people — is our tragedy as well.

So — the Kachinas left us, but they did not forget us. They are supposed to man the unknown objects which in our time haunt our atmosphere by night as by day. Now in this last phase they neither instruct nor warn us. They watch us and surely will see to it that the few chosen people will be safely guided through the breakdown of our civilization. These few have been chosen to impart a new spiritual philosophy to mankind — afterwards.

Josef Blumrich: *Kasskara und die Sieben Welten*
Econ Verlag, Postfach 9229, D-4000 Düseldorf 1, W. Germany
Josef Blumrich: 1139 Noria Str., Laguna Beach, CA 92651, USA

It has been very exciting to work with this material. As you can probably all feel, it is something which you just don't get through from one day to the other.

With the books of George Adamski in front of you I can urge you to go on and read the Kasskara book. The information given is as valuable as the information given in the Adamski books. To compare, one could say that the information given by Adamski is part of daily life, not only in our time, but also way back behind oceans of time. I am grateful and overwhelmed to have been given the opportunity to read *Kasskara and the Seven Worlds*, and I just hope that you may all get the same opportunity. In *Kasskara and the Seven Worlds* you will find the whole modern UFO-case unrolled before your eyes with its observations, landings, contacts, teleportations, bi-location, telepathy, healing and so on as part of daily life in older days and told and given to us as the most natural things in this world by one of the few remaining genuine cosmic people — White Bear Frederics, born 1905 in the Hopi reservation of Old Oraibi, Arizona, U.S.A.   *H. C. Petersen*

79

CONTACT IN HOPILAND

Fred Pulver lives with his wife, Delores who has also had UFO experiences, and six children, one of whom reported a UFO experience recently, in a small town in Colorado. Fred's training is in nutritional counselling (macrobiotics) and he is director of a non-profit foundation dedicated to help research/education. He is also trained in hypnotherapy, iridology and research of aging mechanisms.

— Pulver, in *Contact in Hopiland*, describes his own personal encounters with the UFO beings in connection with the prophecies yet to come.

"They have been here," I thought, overwhelmed by a sense of past contacts between the people of Hopiland and aliens from other planets.

The feeling was in the rocks, in the houses, everywhere. I had been invited to stay with an elderly couple in Hotevilla, one of the most traditional villages on the Hopi reservation in northern Arizona, one summer around 1973, as a guest and friend.

It was so quiet there, with no cars, radios, TV, or city noise to speak of. A strange sense of timelessness pervaded the atmosphere, reassuring and comforting. I needed that, since my heart had just been broken by family problems, and the timeless sense seemed to make me dwell in the ever-present moment rather than the past.

The effect was to wipe away the pain in my heart and keep me from becoming depressed by recent personal difficulties. I welcomed the peaceful atmosphere of Hopiland like a soothing balm for my soul, and found myself able to think, sort out, detach from my life as I had not been able to do for some time.

One afternoon when the sense of the imminent presence of UFO aliens was especially strong, I was drawn to the edge of the village overlooking the vast plain that stretched into the distant haze for miles.

I felt a strong conviction that I could telepathically communicate with UFO-nauts if I just concentrated hard enough. So I started focusing my mind on the thought that I would like very much to establish contact with UFO aliens.

After exhausting myself with this effort, I waited for a response. Not getting any, I decided to return to the house of the couple I was staying with and rest, as the heat of the day was approaching.

Inside the stone house, it was cool. I sat on the window sill admiring the whitewashed purity of the house next door, while a gathering of Hopi gentlemen commiserated in a language I could not understand about their problems while demolishing a large watermelon.

Suddenly, as if someone turned on a radio inside my head, I distinctly heard a male, authoritative voice, almost military in its clipped manner, ask, "Would you like to meet someone from a flying saucer?"

Quite astonished, almost without thinking, I thought back, "Why, of course." The same voice tersely replied, "Then wait until after dinner tonight." Then the voice and the strange "carrier wave" it included, ceased abruptly, like turning off a radio.

Well, I thought the heat must have gotten the best of me, for sure, or I had overtaxed my brain and was hallucinating. But on second thought, I decided to wait until after dinner to pass judgment on the preceding episode.

The sense of timelessness returned and I promptly forgot the strange communication that had just occurred.

Late afternoon faded into evening. The stars came out. I had returned after dinner to the same window ledge I had occupied earlier in the day. As I again listened to the melodious sounds of the Hopi tongue as it rolled from the gathering of men and women who had stopped by to visit my host family, I experienced once again the strange sense of a radio being turned on inside my brain.

Again a male voice with a clipped, military-like precision announced, "Now is the time. Go out the door and walk up the hill." Startled, I jumped up without hesitation and walked out the door, not even questioning the command I had heard so clearly inside my mind.

There was a gentle slope outside the front door leading upward, which I had forgotten. As I approached the top of the hill, I noticed two little Hopi children, a boy and a girl of about 4 or 5 years old, facing away from me. They were looking upward and the little boy, with arm raised, finger pointing toward the night sky, said, "Look, up there! There it is!" This struck me as peculiar.

As I looked upward, I saw a point of white light moving from left to right, 30 degrees down from zenith, slowly across the black night sky studded with stars.

My mind immediately attempted to identify it as an airplane (but there was no sound), then as a satellite (but it was too close), and then as a meteorite (no, it was moving too slowly).

As this rapid process of hypothesis and rejection was occurring, I was suddenly struck by an overwhelming, indescribable feeling of love, unlike anything I had ever before experienced, or have ever experienced since. It hit me like a wave of energy and planted itself as a seed-thought transmission within my mind, with a message that I can only explain as all-at-once, but detailed in a linear, sequential fashion, which it was not at all. So much for the limits of our sense of time/space continuum!

The sensation of love awoke a great longing in my heart to join the beings from which such a wonderful feeling emanated. It was like a tenfold magnification of the greatest sense of brotherly love you may have experienced. To me, it was how I imagine it must have felt to meet Jesus when He walked among us.

In any case, the message that was wrapped up inside the wave of love was something like the following — roughly in the order of realization/unfoldment as it occurred to my thought processes:

"Greetings! We are your brothers from space who are hereby establishing contact with you. Your planet is in grave danger. You yourself should not stay on the Hopi reservation any longer, for you are incurring karmic bonds of obligation which you will find harder and harder to break as time continues to pass for you here. Your path of life is much different than the path chosen by the Hopi. Their struggles are not yours, and they will involve you if you stay any longer. Remember why you were born."

Well, I was so totally dazzled by the contact that I could not gather my wits sufficiently to do any remembering of any such deeply significant request. As if sensing my befuddlement, my mind again was penetrated by an energy emanation. Suddenly I could visualize myself in space coming into bodily existence with the express intent to help save humanity and bring peace to Earth.

A telepathic male voice then asked, "And what have you found to be vital to the creation of peace and salvation of humanity?"

Surely and quickly I realized the thrust of my life. What I had found was Yin and Yang, the dynamic principle of change. When understood fully it could enable anyone to master change rather than be a helpless victim of ignorance of the Laws of Change.

As I ruminated thusly, the voice then stated, "The Hopi have their own path of life, which does not yet include the comprehension of this principle. So you must leave. Tomorrow morning we will send someone around to give you a ride back to where your came from. You must return to your own people."

I had just come from Los Angeles, and I did not really want to return, as my experiences there were not very pleasant and I felt some anxiety at the thought of going back there.

Picking up again on my thoughts, the space brother telepathed, "Don't worry. We are now connected spiritually. When ever you are in a bind and feel trapped, just call on me. In fact, we will always be with you, monitoring your life. Continue to teach others fearlessly, explaining what you believe is important to save your planet from destruction. If your planet becomes uninhabitable, we will come down and transport you to another world where you can escape Earth's holocaust."

Sensing a longing I barely allowed to form in my consciousness, the voice went on, "It is not correct now for you to make physical contact with us or ride in our craft, as this would alter your life path too drastically. Do not worry, however.

Many of the medicine men were aware of the spirit realm and of other-wordly visitors.

We will be here whenever you need our help."

A thought I was barely aware of was also answered. "We are helping your people on Earth by subconsciously influencing by telepathic transmissions those in positions of power and influence to divert their minds from destructive designs and plans. However, this is only to delay the confrontations which could mean the end of life on Earth. The real change must come from you and others like you who see a clear vision of a healthier, saner, and more peaceful way of life that all can live in mutual respect and brotherly love. Continue to do all you can toward these ends."

At this point, the transmissions ended abruptly. I returned to my bed which was received like an old friend, and slept peacefully and soundly.The next morning a young couple came by, and again, a recognition sprang up in my awareness that these people were the ones who were "sent" to pick me up. After greeting them I asked if they were going on to Los Angeles. They responded affirmatively and asked if I needed a ride. I accepted, seeing the transmission of the previous evening coming true as had been stated.

The couple said they had seen a UFO from a very short range when I asked them. This confirmed a growing conviction I had been cultivating that 1) sightings are not accidental, for the most part, but intentional on the part of the UFO voyagers, 2) sightings enable telepathic contact to take place, either consciously or unconsciously, or some of both, 3) all those persons who have seen UFOs are connected in a psychic network, 4) one function of this network is to assist each other in a great work 5) this work is nothing less than the transformation of Earth from an endangered planet to a paradise for all life, 6) the UFOnauts were acting as psychic coordinators, assisting all those who are dedicated in any way toward making Earth a better place for all to live.

Such conclusions on my part have been borne out by discussions with persons who have reported UFO sightings. I would like to hear from anyone who has had a UFO experience to verify or rebut the six conclusions expressed above.

An interesting epilogue to my story is that another person, a young man, came by after the young couple forgot to take me with them. Without saying a word to him, he asked if I needed a ride anywhere. I said, "Yes." He waited as we said fond goodbyes and drove me off the reservation in his old pickup truck. I had no trouble getting back to Los Angeles from that point on.

From time to time, I still feel the intervention of "space brothers" in my life, but that is in itself another story. Also significant to me are the experiences of my wife-to-be regarding UFOs, as well as those of my oldest daughter—again, another story, to be told at another time.

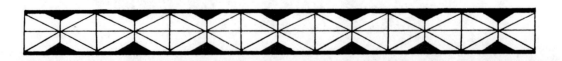

SIGHTINGS OF BIGFOOT REVIVE HOPI LEGEND OF TRIBAL GOD

The connection between the creature commonly referred to as Bigfoot that has been sighted throughout the United States (yes, even in the eastern states!) and legends of the various Amerindian tribes has long been known by students of UFOs as well as the strange and unknown. Brad Steiger came across an old manuscript which dates these occurrences near the reservations back over one hundred years. Many of the Indians we have spoken with take these creatures for granted and do not seem frightened by their frequent appearance. Some, in fact, even see them as a good omen. Good or bad, their reality is now hard to dispute as attested to in this article supplied by UFO Contact International from pages of the Arizona Republic.

A "large hairy, humanoid creature with incredibly big feet," has been reported sighted in recent weeks near Polacca, a Hopi Indian village at the foot of the reservation's First Mesa, according to an article written by Maggie Wilson, published in the Arizona Republic.

According to Kendrick Outah, who first reported the sightings in Qua Toqti, a Hopi newspaper, all who have had a close encounter with the creature are "public figures, reliable people."

Others call it Hairy Harry, or the Incredible Hulk, but some elders of the tribe have another more fearsome name for the apparition. . .MASAU-U. . .one of the gods of the Hopi pantheon. For the traditional Hopi that name alone makes the now eerie events even more disturbing. For knowledgeable "Pahanas" (the Hopi word

for Anglos), the name MASAU-U brings a degree of esoteric fascination to the story that far surpasses the Bigfoot legends.

Outah said the first sightings occurred at Polacca's Assembly of God Church and he reported the thing "caused every dog in the village to begin barking simultaneously," disrupting church services.

The Hopi Tribal Police were called, Outah said, and found smears of fresh blood on the church bus and tracked footprints, "unusually large" but otherwise like human footprints, down the Polacca Wash. But the footprints disappeared where First Mesa's sheer cliffs make their precipitous rise.

Another sighter told Outah that he heard strange noise in the night and, going to investigate, he saw a "very large and hairy living thing" standing beside the shadow of a tree trunk. Again over-sized footprints were found. Again the footprints disappeared at the edge of the mesa by the ancient village of Walpi.

A third sighting occurred in the light of the January 13th full moon, heralded by the barking of dogs gone berserk. When a Hopi husband went to the window he said he saw the being standing near his house. "It ran toward the west and disappeared from sight." Other Hopis have claimed similar experiences (including one who noted that the creature had a head as big as a large pumpkin), but said Outah, "These three sightings have been substantiated by police officers who were dispatched at the sighter's request for assistance."

But the suspicions persist among may Hopis, especially the older ones, that they are seeing the manifestations of a major deity—MASAU-U, the god who controls the underworld, death and darkness. "There is a certain being at First Mesa whom it could be," a Hopi man cautiously volunteered. "Because of the way life is now, this being might be showing himself to tell the people to shape up and settle down to living the Hopi way." Among many Hopi, that's the general idea — that MASAU-U is reappearing to warn them. MASAU-U has been described as the antithesis of the bright living world of the Hopi. A fearsome creature of the night who wears a large blood-smeared Kachina mask and a rabbit skin robe, he can, according to legend, pass back and forth through the plane of the living and the dead. He is the only Kachina deity who can appear at any time of the year, not just the period between winter solstice and summer solstice when other Kachina appear.

"Though the Kiva, the underground ceremonial chamber, and the grave are his domain, his appearance is not always the fearsome creature of the night. In day, according to legend, he can transform his appearance and can be distinguished from any other handsome young Hopi man only by the incredible length of his feet—roughly the length of a normal man's forearm.

So are the recent Bigfoot sightings in the First Mesa's villages really the result of a kiva priest donning MASAU-U mask and rabbit skin robe and taking it upon himself to warn backsliders from the Hopi Way? "In my experience, things aren't done that way among the Hopis. The manifestation of MASAU-U would be regarded more as a divine revelation but I hate to hazard even that guess. Hopis see, do, hear and think things that make complete sense within the framework of their own culture.

They believe they've seen the creature. I'll let it go at that."

Bigfoot is considered by some Indian tribes to be a sacred being. Its prints (see above photo of plaster of paris cast) have been found on reservations in Canada and the United States.

UFO STORIES of the NORTHWESTERN INDIANS

We don't know a great deal about the author of this chapter, Richard Hack, other than the fact that he has published a number of articles in the now defunct *Flying Saucers* magazine as well as *Exploring the Unknown*. This is in our opinion, one of the most documented proofs that UFOs seem to be especially attracted to the Indians of the Northwest as well as other regions of our proud land. The sightings have been frequent and numerous and continue to this day throughout many of the reservations as attested to in the chapters in this book. The chapter was supplied by Aileen Edwards of UFO Contact International.

The UFO story began many centuries ago, perhaps even predating the coming of man. We have accounts in the Bible, from the Egyptians, and in the pictorial writing of the Stone Age. And in the United States, we have the legends of the American Indian, from North to South, East to West.

I came across the following tales in a book published by the University of Oklahoma Press and written by the Professor Emeritus of English at Washington State University, Ella E. Clark. Entitled *Indian Legends of the Northern Rockies*, it records the creation myths and ancient legends of the Indian tribes that lived in what are now the states of Montana, Wyoming, Idaho, and Washington. Because of the number of legends that could be related to the UFO field, I have decided to concentrate mainly on those involving the

"Little People" — creatures very similar to our modern-day "UFOnauts." I would further point out that the author herself makes no attempt or suggestion at a connection, and that the concepts advanced in this article are my own.

The legends are from the story-tellers of the following tribes: Group 1: the Nez Perces, the Flatheads, the Kalispeis, and the Coeur d'Alenes; Group 2: the Arapaho, the Gros Ventres, the Blackfeet, the Crow, the Assiniboine; the Sioux; Group 3: the Shoshone, the Bannocks, the Kutenais.

Group 1 were Plateau Indians, dwelling in the country of eastern Washington, Oregon, Montana and much of Idaho. Their staple food was the salmon. They lived in communal houses in winter, in simple lean-tos during summer.

Group 2 were the Plains Indians living from the Rockies eastward to the

Mississippi and as far south as Texas. The buffalo was their staple diet and was also used for just about everything else including clothing. The Indians of these tribes travelled by foot until the introduction of the horse during the first half of the 18th century, and since they were the rovers, this meant that they were in fact a hardy people.

Group 3 were also Plains Indians. In addition, they were Plateau Indians as they were representative of neither exclusively.

For our purposes, it must be noted that the tribes listed above are invariably described as composed of extremely intelligent and extremely honest individuals, with the possible exception of the warlike Blackfeet. Further, it should be noted that the Indian has a peculiarly retentive memory and, of course, respect for their ancestors led to the careful preservation of the stories quoted.

Nearly every tribe in the Rockies had some legends about the "Little People." Most detailed and typical are those of the Nez Perces, who called these strange dwarfs "The Stick Indians" because they lived in deep forests. The legends usually went as follows:

The Stick Indians were about 3 ft. in height and formed very much like humans. They wore deer skins, and lived in the deep forests, although they roamed far and wide. Often at night they made strange sounds. They were reputed to be able to turn invisible by rubbing themselves with a certain type of grass. They could hoot exactly like owls or howl exactly like coyotes. They were possessed of incredible strength — an old white man told an Indian once that he had seen a dwarf walking off with a calf under each arm.

They had a habit of invading Indian homes and demanding food, with dire consequences for those who refused. On pg. 50 of this reference book by Miss Clark, a story is related how one evening a hunting party was camped for the night during which a storm blew up. The narrator's uncle ordered the members of the party to cover themselves with blankets, for "A strange visitor is coming." The narrator's father peeked out and saw a little man with long hair, dressed in deerskins. The creature demanded food which was given to him. The next day, however, the narrator's father wound up with a face swollen, presumably as punishment for having peeked at the little man. It is interesting to note the swelling feature, as it is often reported today by witnesses of close-range UFO sightings.

Another parallel is to be noted in the fact that the Stick People often kidnapped children. Once, during the last few decades, a party was huckleberrying in the hills. They locked a baby in the car for safe-keeping. While picking berries, the child was heard to cry. It was discovered that he had disappeared. When the cry was heard again, the child was found some distance away. Something had removed him from the locked car—the Indians ascribed the act to the Little People.

The Flatheads described the Little People as about 3 ft. tall, with very dark skins, apparently darker than the Indians' own skins. Strangely, the Little People were reputed to own herds of tiny horses less then 3 ft. in height. These horses were not used for packing or riding but in winter were killed for food.

The Coeur d'Alenes report that many dwarfs lived around Rosebud Lake which was surrounded by dense brush. They had the odd habit of beating sticks against the trunks of trees. Some were dressed in squirrel skins and some were described as being users of the bow and arrow. They had a habit of shouting when they saw strangers, thus drawing hunters on to wild goose chases, much like the strange lights that today hover over roads and deserted areas across the country, luring police and others away from such places.

The Shoshone and the Bannocks had many legends about the Ninnimbe, the "Little Demons." These were supposed to haunt the areas near the source of Muddy Creek, Wyoming. They, like the others, were between 2 and 3 ft. tall, very strong, and dressed in goatskin clothing. They were expert stalkers and hunters, and were described as fearless. Very interesting is the concept of the invisible poison arrows with which they killed game and many a Shoshone. They were reported to have done the carvings on the rocks in the Wind River country. The Indians had a curious defense which consisted of putting on a great deal of paint, for the Little People were supposedly afraid of paint.

One of the Little People allegedly still survives. He, too, is called Ninnimbe. He is described as an old man, sturdily built, dressed in brightly-painted skins. His nose, like Rudolph's, is red. He lives in the mountains, appearing and disappearing at will. Stone darts have been found which have been attributed to him.

The dwarfs are reported to be cannibalistic in the legends of the Shoshone and Bannocks. The descriptions are the same, as well as the reported great physical strength. But the creatures had the disconcerting and somewhat gruesome habit of eating children and their mothers. The Little Men would seize a child, devour it, then perfectly imitate the cry of the child to lure its parents. When the Indian woman was seized, her screams usually frightened the being off, but the women usually died before morning. The Little Men also would creep up on a party of children, hide their tails by wrapping them around their bodies and request to play with the children. They would then seize a child, perch him on their tails and run off, never to be seen again. Curiously enough, these cannibals would never eat men. Instead, they would invite them into their homes and offer them food.

The Little People of the Arapaho, Gros Ventres, and Blackfeet were again 3 ft. high, with black skins and big stomachs, powerfully built. They were versed in a crude sign language and reportedly carved the rock houses in the deep canyons in Wyoming, Northeast Minnesota, and Montana. Some houses and skeletons remain in these areas, according to the Indians. The creatures were also far fleeter runners than the swiftest Indian, as well as being incredibly strong, and, here too, cannibalistic. These tribes tried to kill off the Little People, but arrows had no effect, so they were forced to herd the enemy into a deep gorge, drive them to the trees, and set fire to them, destroying them all.

Then there is the story of the Medicine Wheel, a photograph of which is included in the book. This strange construction, located in the Big Horn Mountains west of Sheridan, Wyoming, is composed of thousands of limestone slabs laid in a

Much of the ritualistic wardrobe of the various North American tribes may represent vague remembrances of space suits worn by the Star Gods who visited in times past.

wheel form 245 ft. in diameter. There are 28 or 29 spokes radiating from it. On some of the slabs, buffalo skulls look to the east.

A story is told about Red Plume, a famous Crow Indian chief, which goes to the effect that he once went to the Medicine Wheel and stayed there four nights and four days. On the fourth night, he was visited by three little men and a little woman. They conducted him to a hidden underground passage beneath the Medicine Wheel. He remained with them for three days and three nights, learning the arts of war and how to be a good leader. This story backs up the belief that the Indians tell: that the Little People lived once in the rock shelters to be found near the strange monument.

The above stories are the majority to be found in Miss Clark's book, but by no means all. It is interesting to note the strange relationships these tales have with the ones heard today from the sober lips of businessmen, police officers, and others who have encountered these strange creatures — or ones like them.

For instance, it is a fact that quite a few stories of "babies crying" have been reported to have occurred in cemeteries, supposedly haunted houses, etc. And here we have the Shoshone telling us that this is a technique to lure small children from their mothers, to be devoured.

The incredible strength has been reported by several South American witnesses, as has the apparent invulnerability to simple weapons like knives.

The entire area of the creatures' interest in children today leads to the gruesome conjectures when related to the cannibal stories of yesterday. And the disappearance of young men and teenagers — is there any reason to believe that we are little more than a stockyard for sub-human races? I think this latter answer is too limited, but we must consider the possibility that some few missing children may have indeed been murdered, and that others may have narrowly escaped this fate and lived to describe their meeting with these "abominable little men."

I would suggest in conclusion that an effort be made to investigate the areas described by the Northern Rockies Indian tribes as abodes of the Little People. It may be that remains might be found indicating the fate of these beings over the years. It might also be reasonable to quietly find out what is happening in these areas with regard to the UFO phenomenon itself.

I suggest that researchers in the Northwest take the time to visit the Medicine Wheel, the Owyhee Range, the Salmon and Wind River countries, and investigate the occurrences there, particularly the incidence of "cattle rustling," or kidnappings, as well as straight UFO and contactee reports. It may be that the little creatures that plagued the Ancient Indian are even now plaguing modern man, using far more advanced techniques and perhaps under the auspices of a new master —the "Alien."

(Editor's Note: Pat McGuire was taken to the Medicine Wheel near Sheridan, Wyoming during his abduction by UFOnauts. He was let out and walked around to see where he was; picked up and taken back to near Laramie, Wyoming where his ranch was.)

CULTIVATING THE STARSEED CONNECTION

What is the actual connection between UFOs and the American Indian tribes? Astute thinker, Brad Steiger, poses many thoughtful questions and provides provocative answers to this very intriguing idea, posing the theory that extraterrestrials have chosen the Hopi as well as other tribes to be their representatives today just as they have done over a great period of time.

In the minds of orthodox archaeologists and anthropologists, the origins of the Amerindian have been clearly charted: sporadic migrations of people crossed from Siberia into Alaska over a period of more than 15,000 years. Before these Siberians invaded the New World, the continent was like the Garden of Eden without an Adam or an Eve.

Most of the Amerindians with whom I have discussed the matter of the origins of the Indian people upon this continent simply do not accept the Bering Strait invasion theory as the true account of their genesis. They do not deny that such an invasion took place any more than they deny that the European invasion took place, but they do not believe that their origins were in Siberia any more than that they came from England or France.

The physical makeup of certain tribes, especially those of the far west, bear mute testimony that interbreeding occurred between Amerindian and Mongolian types, just as nearly all tribes bear evidence of interbreeding with Europeans. But the traditional Amerindian strongly maintains that just as various tribes were here to welcome the European, so were they already on these shores to greet the Siberian. The Amerindian peoples, they believe, are the descendants of those who survived the destruction of a great civilization which once existed on this continent. And they believed this long before the sleeping prophet Edgar Cayce declared that the inhabitants of lost Atlantis were a red-skinned people.

ANCIENT ARTIFACTS

For one thing, the people who came over from Siberia were primitive. How then, utilizing the orthodox timetable, does one explain the sophisticated stone tools found in an ancient Mexican stream bed, which were considerably more advanced than those used in Europe and Asia 250,000 years ago? The most primitive tools found in the stream bed were of a type used in the Old World 35,000 to 40,000 years ago.

"We have apparently found geological data that lead to a head-on confrontation with apparently sound archaeological data," Dr. Ronald Fryxwell of Washington State University was quoted as saying in the *New York Times*, Nov. 18, 1973.

Even more dramatic than finding sophisticated stone tools that may be 250,000 years old are the various walled cities and fortifications which have been found scattered throughout the U.S.

In Rockwall, Texas' smallest county, four square miles support the great stone walls of an ancient fortification—some of which are 49 feet high and eight inches thick. The stones have been placed on top of each other with the ends breaking near the center of the stone above or below, just as an expert mason would build a wall. The stones give the appearance of having been beveled around their edges.

Raymond B. Cameron told Frank Tolbert, columnist for the *Dallas Morning News*, that "four large stones taken from wall segments appear to have been inscribed by some form of writing."

In the 1920s, a visiting archaeologist declared that the walled city appeared remarkably similar to the buried cities he had excavated in North Africa and the Middle East.

Cherokee Indians, ancient Welshmen, and a vanished tribe of moon-eyed, blond-haired whites have at various times been credited with the construction of the 885-foot-long wall on Fort Mountain in northern Georgia. The wall runs from east to west and at various intervals looms over 29 pits that look as though they might have served as ancient foxholes. The wall ranges from a height of seven feet to only two to three. The quantity of rock along the wall suggests that the fortification might once have been much higher.

According to John Fleming, writing in *Southern Living*, December 1969: "The lack of warlike artifacts (or any artifacts for that matter) lends credence to the old Cherokee legend that the wall was built by a race of white people who worshipped the sun. This, according to the tale, is why the wall was built from east to west — from the rising sun to the setting sun.

"But if this is true, then what happened to the sun worshippers? How did they leave the area without leaving a trace of artifacts or funerary remains?"

On June 27, 1969, workmen leveling a rock shelf at 122nd Street on the Broadway Extension between Edmond and Oklahoma City, Okla, uncovered a rock formation that created a great deal of controversy among investigating authorities. To the layman, the site looked like an inlaid mosaic tile floor.

"I am sure this was man-made because the stones are placed in perfect sets of parallel lines which intersect to form a diamond shape, all pointing to the east," said Durwood Pate, an Oklahoma City geologist who studied the site. "We found post holes which measure a perfect two rods from the other two. The top of the stone is very smooth, and if you lift one, you will find it is very jagged, which indicates wear on the surface. Everything is too well placed to be a natural formation [*Edmond Booster*, July 3, 1969]"

Delbert Smith, a geologist and president of the Oklahoma Seismograph Company, said the formation, which was discovered about three feet beneath the surface, appeared to cover several thousand square feet. The *Tulsa World* (June 29, 1969) quoted Smith as saying: "There is no question about it. It has been laid there, but I have no idea by whom."

On Dec. 17, 1869, the *Los Angeles News* printed the following account:

"Captain Lacy of Hammondsville, Ohio, had some men engaged in making an entry into his coal bank, when a huge mass of coal fell down, disclosing a large, smooth slate wall, upon the surface of which were plainly carved several lines of hieroglyphics. No one has yet been able to tell in what language the words are written. The letters are raised; the first line contains 25. It is probable that they were cut in the coal while in its vegetable state and during its formation into coal."

The men discovered the wall with its undecipherable hieroglyphics about 100 feet below the surface. If the letters were cut into the coal in its "vegetable state," as the anonymous reporter suggested, then we're back in the Carboniferous Systems, approximately *250 million years ago*.

UNORTHODOX TIMETABLE

In 1973 and 1974, the following confrontations with the orthodox timetable for the beginnings of human habitation on this continent were recorded by archaeologists:

■ The amino-acid dating of a human skull found in California indicates human habitation of North America 50,000 years ago;

■ The oldest discovered site of human habitation east of the Mississippi—14,000 to 15,000 years ago—was uncovered south of Pittsburgh, Pa.;

■ The mysterious Medicine Wheel in Wyoming's Bighorn Mountains was discovered to have astronomical alignment and may have been used as an observatory by nomadic Plains Indians;

■ A carved bone hide scraper, found on the Old Crow River, a few miles from the Alaskan border, was radiocarbon-dated at 25,000 - 32,000 years old.

Certain archaeologists and anthropologists might have to swallow a pet theory or two, but most would be able to accept the above discoveries with a minimum of pain. After all, 50,000 years can be endured; but the suggestion of humans walking about writing on North American walls 250 million years ago, simply subjects the orthodox thinkers to more shocks than can be comfortably handled.

But consider the following footprints in the geologic strata of Time:

In the early 1930s, Dr. Wilbur Greely Burroughs, head of the Geology Department of Berea College, Kentucky was guided to a site in the Kentucky hills where he was able to locate 10 complete manlike tracks and parts of several more in Carboniferous sandstone. All the accumulated evidence indicates that they were impressed upon a sandy beach in the Pennsylvanian Period of the Paleozoic Era—which dates the humanoid impressions somewhere around *250 million* years ago. Dr. Burroughs kept his work secret for seven years. One can imagine that he wanted every opportunity to study the amazing tracks.

"Three pairs of tracks show both left and right footprints," Dr. Burroughs told Kent Previette of the *Louisville Courier-Journal* many years later (May 24, 1953). "Of these, two pairs show the left foot advanced relative to the right. The position of the feet is the same as that of a human being. The distance from heel to heel is 18 inches. One pair shows the feet about parallel to each other, the distance between the feet being the same as that of a normal human being."

Regardless of the tests to which Dr. Burroughs subjected the tracks, the results were always the same; the footprints were genuinely those of a bipedal creature. It positioned its feet like a human, had a heel and five toes, and walked exclusively on its hind legs.

At the suggestion of Dr. Frank Thone, biology editor of Science Service, with the concurrence of Charles Gilmore of the Smithsonian Institution, Dr. Burroughs named the originator of the mysterious tracks *Phenanthropus mirabilis* ("looks human; remarkable").

The Pennsylvanian Period was the age of giant amphibians. Could the tracks have been caused by one of them?

Dr. Burroughs thought it unlikely. "There is no indication of front feet, through the rock is large enough to have shown front feet if they had been used in walking." Dr. Burroughs was emphatic that the creatures, whatever they might have been, walked on their hind legs. Nowhere on the site were there signs of belly or tail marks.

Is it possible that ancient Amerindian artisans or more contemporary sculptors could have carved those footsteps?

A sculptor informed Dr. Burroughs that any carving done in that kind of sandstone would be certain to leave telltale artificial markings. Neither enlarged photomicrographs nor enlarged infrared photographs revealed any "indications of carving or cutting of any sort."

On May 25, 1969, the *Tulsa Sunday World* carried an article describing fossilized footprints found by Troy Johnson, a North American Rockwell liaison engineer. A few miles beyond Tulsa's eastern city limits, Johnson removed earth, roots, and stone from an outcropping of sandstone to find animal prints—many of which he could not identify—and some distinctive five-toed humanlike footprints.

More than just a weekend dabbler in archaeology, Johnson had 13 years experience in study and field work for, among others, the University of Oklahoma and the University of Arkansas. At the time of his startling discovery he had also presented papers on his finds to archaeological associations.

C. H. McKennon of the *Tulsa Sunday World* presented Troy Johnson's argument in favor of the footprints' authenticity:

"The chunk of sandstone containing the big prints is a massive weight of an estimated 15 tons, which rules out the possibility of someone transporting it to the top of the hill. Also, the stone is of the same strata as other specimens of sandstone dotting the hilltop, indicating there was a monumental 'uplift' of the Earth's crust ages ago..."

If the Coso artifact is what it appears to be, it seems that someone was riding as well as walking, on the North American

Some researchers theorize that various pictographs and Indian carvings of folk gods and spirits actually represent Star Gods or Kachinas.

ontinent eons before any kind of technology was born in Europe and Asia.

On Feb. 13, 1961, Wallace A. Lane, Mike Mikesell, and Virginia Maxey set out for the Coso Mountains six miles northeast of Olancha, Calif., in hopes of finding some semiprecious specimens for their LM & V Rockhounds Gem and Gift Shop. Instead, they found what may be a clue to a precataclysmic world.

At first no one recognized the object as anything other than a geode. It was picked up along with a number of stones near the top of a peak approximately 4,300 feet above sea level and about 340 feet above the dry bed of Owens Lake.

But the next day, back in his workshop, Mikesell ruined his practically new 10-inch diamond saw blade when he cut the fossil-encrusted geode in half.

This geode did not contain a cavity as so many geodes do, but a perfectly circular section of a very hard material that appeared to be ceramic with a two-millimeter shaft of bright metal in its center.

The inner third of the crust seemed composed of a substance resembling petrified wood, but it was somewhat softer than agate or jasper. This layer was hexagonal and seemed to form a casing around the hard ceramic disc. The metal core of the disc responded to a magnet. There also appeared to be some evidence that the ceramic core had been encased in copper, because some of the metal seemed intact while the rest had decomposed.

What was Mrs. Maxey's opinion of the object within the rock?

"One possibility is that it is barely 100 years old—something that lay in a mud bed, then got baked and hardened by the sun in a matter of a few years." (However, Mrs. Maxey supplied the information that in the opinion of a trained geologist who examined the fossil shells encrusting it, the nodule had taken *at least 500,000 years to attain its present form*.) "Or else it is an instrument as old as legendary Mu or Atlantis. Perhaps it is a communication device or some sort of direction finder or some instrument made to utilize power principles we know nothing about."

AN ANCIENT SPARK PLUG

When Ron Calais did the basic research on the Coso artifact for the *INFO Journal*, editor Paul J. Willis accepted the challenge to come up with an idea of what the object might have been. After examining X-ray photos of the geode and doodling a bit with his pencil, Willis said that the hexagonal part reminded him of a *spark plug!*

Then Willis and his brother Ron tried to saw a common spark plug in half near its hexagon. They soon found the porcelain was too hard for their hacksaw, but they did manage to get the plug apart.

"We found the components similar to the Coso artifact," Ron Willis writes, "but with some differences. The copper ring around the halves displayed in the object seems to correspond to a copper sealer ring in the upper part of the steel casing of any spark plug."

They believe that the hexagonal area in the geode is probably composed of rust, the remains of a steel casing. The Willis brothers noted that the central shaft of the spark plug they had taken apart had a tint which reminded them of brass.

The upper end of the object appears to end in a spring, but Ron and Paul theorized that what is seen in the X-ray photograph might be "the remains of a corroded piece of metal with threads."

Although the large metallic piece in the upper section of the Coso artifact may not seem to correspond exactly with a contemporary spark plug, the overall effect is certainly that of some kind of electrical apparatus. If it is some bizarre trick of Nature, it is indeed a good one.

There are numerous other artifacts indicative of an advanced precataclysmic technology on the North American continent. I recount the details of several of them in my book *Mysteries of Time and Space*. Among the evidence of a prehistoric industrialized society is the following intriguing discovery:

In 1953, miners of the Lion coal mine of Wattis, Utah broke into a network of tunnels between five and six feet in height and width, which contained coal of such vast antiquity that it had become weathered to a state of uselessness for any kind of burning. A search outside the mountain in direct line with the tunnels revealed no sign of any entrance. Since the tunnels were discovered when the miners were working an eight-foot-wide coal seam at 8,500 feet below the surface, the evidence is irrefutable that an undetermined person conducted an ambitious mining project so far back in time that all exterior traces have eroded way.

Prof. John E. Wilson of the Department of Engineering, University of Utah, was quoted in the February 1954 issue of *Coal Age* as stating:

"Without a doubt, both drifts were man-made. Though no evidence was found at the outcrop, the tunnels apparently were driven some 450 feet from the outside to the point where the present workings broke into them...There is no visible basis for dating the tunnels..."

Jesse D. Jennings, Professor of Anthropology at the University of Utah, could offer no opinion as to the identify of the ancient miners, but he denied that the vast tunnels and coal mining rooms could have been the work of any Amerindian people.

"In the first place," he commented, "such works would have required immediate and local need for coal... because, before the white man came, transport was by human cargo carriers...As for local use, there was no reported extensive burning of coal by aboriginals in the region of the Wattis mine."

For those who are skeptical that a prehistoric civilization would have thrived on our own continent and left only the slightest vestige of its culture to alert future generations of its existence, consider what would happen if a catastrophe should wipe out our own civilization. What would remain for archaeologists to unearth 15,000 years from now?

We are builders in wood and metal. Our most majestic stone buildings are little more than facades supported by thin tendons of steel. In 1,000 years, even without flood, fire, or nuclear warfare, our major cities would be little more than rubble. Our complex super highways would be crumbled bits of stone beneath layers of vegetation. Our once intricate railway system would merely be red dust blowing in the wind.

If volcanic lava and dust should happen to blanket a major city in a sudden eruption—such as Mt. Vesuvius did to Herculaneum and Pompeii—a portion of our civilization would be preserved as if in a gigantic museum display.

But if we were to enter another ice age and enormous glaciers should creep down from the north, as they have done several times previously in the past million years, everything in their inexorable path would be pulverized. One such glacier would be enough to wipe out any trace of our civilization. Perhaps only scattered pieces of porcelain would remain to inspire future scholars to write doctoral dissertations on what matter of priesthood served which deity at the altar of the flush toilet.

In my own thinking, I have narrowed the matter down to the following, personal analogy: although the Iowa village in which I live is small and several hours away from any large, metropolitan area, we have all the modern conveniences, along with up-to-date shops and supermarkets, a well-staffed hospital, and a small college. Let us hypothesize the unpleasant situation of the entire civilized world blasting itself to nuclear bits. All the major cities are obliterated, but life in small villages such as ours does it best to continue.

The television set is no longer functional, except, perhaps, as something on which to stack books. The radio is functional only until the local station has a breakdown which will necessitate ordering new parts. It is impossible, of course, to order new parts for anything from anywhere. Automobiles are functional only until the storage tanks of gasoline have been exhausted and the local mechanics can no longer improvise repair.

The doctors at the hospital and the clinics do their best to instruct the more intelligent among us in the rudiments of modern medicine; but modern medicine's magic may be very weak without its attendant technology, which has now been destroyed. The teachers and professors at the public schools and the college do their best to keep alive the ideals of our culture; but effective crop raising now seems much more important than philosophy, and survival must take priority over Shakespeare.

The years pass. One day the last machine breaks down, and there is no one who remembers how to repair it. The X-ray machines, the radios, the long-dead dry cell batteries, although still revered, are useless. They will soon be forgotten as actual implements, but they will be elevated to the status of magical artifacts in the legends of the Iowa villagers, as survival instinct sends them back into the rapidly encroaching forests.

Someday, perhaps 20,000 years in the future, someone will "remember" how to use the marvelous machines: the box that could see other people thousands of miles away; the machine that could look through humans; the chariot that could fly through the clouds. Or perhaps someday more technologically sophisticated men and women from across the big water will declare those Iowa villagers to be primitive, aboriginal people of the New World.

Since the concept of "ancient astronauts" has become a popular one in the last few years, it would be only fair to consider briefly that the various artifacts which we have discussed in this article might have been "seeded" on this continent by colonists from other worlds or other dimensions. It is also conceivable that the collective unconscious of the Amerindians may recall their origin in a culture which might be found on some other planet, rather than a "lost civilization" on Earth. Or that same collective unconscious may harbor memories of the intimate interaction of their ancestors with extraterrestrial visitors.

Just as Great Britain had its Stonehenge, Egypt its pyramids, and the Mayans their temples which served as giant calendars as well as impressive monuments, the nomadic Plains Indians of North America had their Big Horn Medicine Wheel to signal the summer solstice—or, perhaps the "gods."

Just above the timberline in the Big Horn Mountains of northern Wyoming, the Medicine Wheel's pattern of stones etches an imperfect circle with a diameter of about 80 feet. A cairn of stones 15 feet in diameter establishes the hub of the wheel. Twenty-eight "spokes" jut out from the hub and connect with the outer rim.

SECRETS OF THE BIG HORN MOUNTAINS

The Big Horn Mountains held special significance for the Crow, the Sioux, the Arapaho, the Shoshone, or the Cheyenne—any of whom might have erected the wheel—but one of these tribes were known for building any kind of stone monuments. Bits of wood found in one of the six smaller cairns situated unevenly about the rim indicates that the Medicine Wheel has been there since at least 1760. The monument has been known to white men for well over 100 years, but conjec-

ture about its true purpose has only inspired mysteries and tall tales.

In the June 7, 1974 issue of *Science*, astronomer John A. Eddy of the High Altitude Observatory in Boulder, Col., states that two summer's research have convinced him that the Big Horn Monument may well have been a primitive astronomical observatory that served its creators at least as well as Stonehenge served its primitive astronomers. The high altitude (9,640 feet) and the clear horizon of the monument make the marking of sunrise and sunset at the summer solstice easily visible. Accurate knowledge of the first day of summer would have been most important information for a nomadic people whose very lives depended on astute awareness of seasonal change.

HOME OF THE GODS

There are numerous Amerindian legends which suggest an interaction between native American peoples and Star Dwellers. Nearly every tribe has its accounts of "Sky Ropes"—ropes of feathers that permitted People From Above to come to the Earth Mother and, on occasion, enabled men and women to fly to the clouds. Along with the magical ropes are tales of flying canoes, airships, and moons that descended to Earth.

Many Amerindian tribes believed that the stars were the homes of higher beings who had a connection with, and a mysterious relationship to, humans. Others held that the stars were themselves actual ministering intelligences.

Numerous tribes had accounts of warriors who had found themselves enamored of Star Wives and of tribes-women who had been enticed by Star Husbands. Often the Amerindians found "magic circles" which the Star People had burned into the grass, just as their European brothers across the ocean were finding "fairy circles" that the dancing elves had tromped into the meadows during their nocturnal revels.

The Chippewa have a legend that tells of a great "star with wings" that hovered over the tree tops. Some of the wise men took it as a precursor of good; others saw it as the forerunner of terrible times.

The star hovered near the village for nearly one moon (month) when a Star Maiden approached a young warrior and told him that she was from the winged star. They had returned from a faraway place to this the land of their forefathers, and they loved the happy race they saw living in the village. The star, she said, wished to live among them.

The warrior told the council of this visitation, and representatives went to welcome the Star People with sweet-scented herbs in their peace pipes. The winged star stayed with them for only a brief time, however, before it left to live in the southern sky. As a token of its eternal love, according to the Chippewa, the Star People left the white water lily on the surface of the lakes.

SASQUATCH

There are literally hundreds of Amerindian legends suggesting a steady line of interaction between the native Americans and the Sky People. There is an episode from the journal of an early cattleman which implies not only an association between the Amerindians and UFOs, but also with that mysterious creature variously called Bigfoot or Sasquatch.

The account was supplied by James C. Wyatt of Memphis, Tenn. In a journal dated 1888, Wyatt's grandfather records that he was somewhere along the Humboldt Line in the "Big Woods Country" where his father and several cowhands had wintered with a tribe of Indians after delivering cattle to a fort farther north.

One day he came upon an Indian carrying a large platter of raw meat. At first the man seemed afraid to answer Wyatt's questions concerning his errand, but he finally asked the cattleman to follow him.

In a shallow cave in a cliff face dwelt a beast with long, shiny black hair that covered its entire body, except for its palms and an area around its eyes. The manlike creature did not seem wild or vicious; it sat cross-legged, Indian-style, to eat the raw meat. Wyatt described the creature as built like a big, well-developed man, except for it lack of neck and its long body hair. The creature's head seemed to rest directly on its shoulders.

"Crazy Bear," as the creature was called by the Indians, had been brought to the "Big Woods" from the stars. A "small moon" had flown down like a swooping eagle and had landed on a plateau a few miles from the Indian's encampment. The beast in the cave and two other "crazy bears" had been flung out of the "moon" before the craft had once again soared off to the stars.

Other "crazy bears" had been left in the vicinity over the years. The Indian villagers had occasionally seen the "men" who dropped the crazy bears form the small moons. They did not look like the giant hairy ones, but appeared to be more like men such as themselves. The men in the small moons had much shorter hair than the Indians, however, and they wore shiny clothing. They always waved to the Indians in a friendly manner before they closed the door in their small moon and flew back to the stars.

The "crazy bears" had been led to the village by the Indians, and at no time had the hairy giants offered any resistance to their benefactors. The Indians believed that the "crazy bears" from the stars had been sent to bring them powerful medicine, and they would not permit the creatures to stray lest they be captured by rival tribes.

Each of the Amerindian tribes I am familiar with cherish legends which tell of their people rising from the destruction which had been visited upon a former civilization. Most of the accounts deal with the surviving peoples having escaped from a terrible flood, immediately suggesting the biblical story of "The Deluge" and the Atlantis myth. The principal point of each of the Amerindian myths of destruction and rebirth is that civilization is cyclical, continually being born, struggling toward a golden age, slipping backward into a moral morass, forward into its death throes, only to be reborn so that the process may begin again.

Immanuel Velikovsky once said in an interview with *Science and Mechanics* magazine that prior civilizations are buried so deeply within the lower strata of the Earth that we simply do not have archaeological evidence of their existence.

"But," he stated, "we have abundant references in literature—even in rabbinical literature—that many times, before this present Earth Age existed, the *same* Earth was created—then leveled and recreated; all civilizations were buried,"

"By far the vast majority of ancient texts deal specifically with the phenomenon of catastrophism. In the Old Testament we read of geological disturbances in which a mountain melts like wax, the sea being torn apart or erupting on the land, cosmic debris bombarding the people, the ocean parting to show the foundations of Earth—and we say all these things are metaphors! This is what makes it appear to me that mankind is a victim of collective amnesia. As such a victim, he likes to play with atomic weapons, then repeat the events that took place! The victim of amnesia who has undergone a traumatic experience seems to want to relive those experiences."

The Seneca legend of the Seven Worlds says that Man has relived such "traumatic experiences" six times before and that we stand on the brink of destruction prior to entering the final world in our evolutionary cycle. The Hopi legend of the Four Worlds agrees and states that mankind is about to enter the final world after a last great war, a war which shall resolve the spiritual with the material and create one world under the power of the Creator.

For the Amerindian traditionalist, the destructions of the previous worlds have been a necessary part of mankind's spiritual evolution. Because man has repeatedly forgotten the lessons of the Great Spirit, the Earth Mother has been periodically cleansed for new epochs. If the old prophecies are correct, we have little time to avoid becoming part of the collective amnesia of some future generation.

VISION AT COURTHOUSE ROCK SEDONA, ARIZONA

David Jungclaus is an international psychic and channel who has adapted himself to the Amerindian ways, using the name Night Hawk to journey forth through various unordinary worlds that can only be reached through shamanic teachings and visions.

Having experienced many astounding UFO sightings, Night Hawk tells about his adventures as a channel that eventually lead him to a very special vision quest in Sedona, Arizona, a vortex area of special mystical importance to the Amerindian tribes who have long populated the area some 100 miles from Phoenix. This is the story of that vision which should be of importance to all of us.

Like many of those who have experienced a close encounter, my contact lay dormant until it was time to fit in with 'The Plan.' This is a term used by the Spacehood and by many UFO contactees when explaining their experiences. It all began when I was prospecting for uranium thirty miles outside Austin, Nevada. I was twenty miles off a small highway staying in a sled metal shack next to an old mining mill. The event took place in this isolated area around 9:30 P.M. one evening. I know the approximate time as it was half an hour after our generator ran out of gas and shut off. My prospecting partner and I were just climbing into bed when we heard a low humming sound. We ran outside and saw a great ball of light move toward us through the valley. It was as if nighttime had turned into day. We stood watching this round light move toward us. It hovered near us for a very long time. I felt no fear but my partner did and he reached for his rifle. Then I became afraid. I knew if he shot at this light we would both be killed. I think he finally sensed that his weapon was only a toy and he set it down.

We could have stood watching the ball for five minutes or two to three hours. I do remember seeing a round silver ship behind the light. I don't remember going to bed. I do remember waking up and hearing a humming sound flying over us, but for some strange reason I rolled over back into sleep. Early that morning we drove the jeep to one of our claims, and on a hill next to it we saw a black burnt top with runner marks embedded in the snow. One looked like sled marks. We told the town sheriff the next day of what we saw and he just laughed.

"Do me a favor. Don't report it to me or they will be asking a lot of questions and then all they are going to say is that it was truck lights you saw or a helicopter from one of the mining companies." I had read, *They Walk Among Us* and believed in the possibility of extraterrestrial beings. This was during the early UFO encounters and the start of military classification, secrecy and "Project Blue Book." Many years later I learned this was my first onboard contact and that they examined and questioned me. Unlike many UFO encounters of the first kind I had no apparent physical, psychological or spiritual change, and I had no bad after effects. Even later when I was allowed to remember I found it to be an unfearful event.

The next part of my 'spiritual destiny' took place after the first two, and it brought those earlier experiences into a profound and logical relationship, deepening and connecting them. This was my first *aware* space contact. It began first through automatic handwriting along with a strong telepathical connection between us. He called himself Star Commander Varcus, from the Mothership *Anderius*. He told me that I had contact with a small craft from a Venus Mothership outside Austin, Nevada and through them he was directed to me. I was to be his first contact with an earth being. We started communicating twice a week at a set time. I soon began channeling Star Commander on my tape recorder. During the night as I slept I was told I was being taught 'Earth History' by telepathic mind programming from the Mothership.

Finally, one night I was beamed aboard the Mothership *Anderius*. It was a very peculiar feeling. One minute I was lying in bed and the next I was materializing on the Mothership. I remember looking down at my feet wondering if I was all together. A group of space beings watched me. Then one of them moved toward me and clasped my shoulders.

"Greetings and Salutations, Thordonious, we of the Mothership *Anderius* welcome you."

The name Thordonious was given to me by Star Commander Varcus. The name Thordonious means beloved, dear one . . . the space counterpart of my given name, David.

I felt a warm surge of love fill me. I felt as if I belonged. After I as given a tour of the complete ship I learned that my biological mother was from outer space and that my biological father was an earth contactee. When I was orphaned at the age of one the Spacehood selected my step-parents and directed them to me. I learned one of my protectors as a child was a dwarf. My wife and I saw the dwarf once sitting in a tall oak tree looking in our bedroom window.

"You have always been monitored," Star Commander Varcus said.

This encounter when I was beamed up was witnessed by my wife, Barbara. She awoke to see a pink ray of light shimmering over my body. She said my eyes were closed and it seemed as if I were not breathing. Suddenly I gave her a start. Air surged from my mouth in a whoosh. My body spasmed a few times and then settled down into normal sleep. My wife was afraid to wake me. Later my wife told me about the pink lights! I remember feeling a lightness of body and it took me several days to ground myself physically.

THE AWARENESS

In a vision my friend Adele was told that her daughter Susie and I were to accompany her to Sedona, Arizona, a place that has always had the highest spiritual importance to several Indian tribes. On arrival we would be guided to where we should go.

A year before I had initiated Adele into the Medicine Wheel. During this time she was given her power, Power Totems and Power Animals. Adele was a very gifted channel and had worked in the psychic field a long time before I met her. Since the first initiation we had worked in the Medicine Wheel together. Adele and Susie were already familiar with Sedona and previously had many wonderful psychic encounters. While I was preparing myself for the initiation at Sedona, Adele was being prepared by Anton, her space contact.

My awareness that something special was to take place came through a vision while in the Medicine Wheel. I saw an Indian woman with a small child sitting on a white buffalo robe in front of a stone-ringed fire. The logs were blazing. The firelight flickered on the cave walls. As I looked at her I saw the start of a sandpainting beside her. She held her hand out to me as if to ask me to join her.

The following night I remember being taken aboard the Mothership *Anderius* and was taught the *Lemurian-Atlantean Bonding Ceremony*. At this time I had no idea why I was given this teaching other than in time they wanted me to be able to perform this ceremony for others.

TRAVELING TO SEDONA

Very early one Saturday morning several years ago, through spiritual guidance Adele and I feel a strong energy. We both feel our energies balancing. The whole house shimmers in a blue light as we ready ourselves for the trip to Sedona. We have made reservations late Friday night after the Bonding and shared channeling. Though it was really too late to make reservations at this time of year, Spirit provided a late cancellation.

In the car, Adele plays light new age music. The fourwheeler vibrates with strong energy that we can all feel. At once we seem connected to those waiting for us. We all see space craft either to the side or above us. Adele channels two of the crafts we see flying side by side. Anton, Adele's contact, is in one craft and Star Commander, my contact, is in another. They tell us everything is ready and once we arrive we will be directed to where we are to meet. Strong love is being beamed to us. *The energy fills our heart chakras* and is so intense that we wonder if we can receive any more.

Adele is told to stop and drive in off the road. A barbed wire fence stops us from driving any further and we get out of the car. The day is sunny and warm. I can tell it had rained a few days ago as the ground has a washed clean look and there are only a few animals prints. Several of the prints were rabbits and a few isolated snakes. I notice a dog print and maybe another one that was a mountain cat. We start along a vague pathway. Brush covers much of it and we had to be careful of the cactus growing out of the

Indians of the Southwest consider Sedona, Arizona to be highly sacred ground.

red clay. Ahead of us in this valley are beautiful mountains. Susie is as great a hiker as her mother and enjoys coming to this area. On other trips they had received wonderful channelings here by themselves and with others.

"This is the spot," Adele seems to sense it more than physically locate it.

It is beautiful. We are standing on a wide high flat sand formation. In front of us the majestic mountain seem to touch the clear blue sky.

"The large red mountain is *Courthouse Rock*," Adele says. The three of us sit down. There is no wind, only silence. The Force has seen to it that we're alone. There are no people, jeeps or horseback riders. This whole vista is ours for this moment in time.

SPIRIT WIND CALLS US

I stand on a ledge facing Courthouse Rock as the sun warms my face. *I listen for the Silent Winds.* Slowly the murmuring earth and sky become still. As the hush covers the land I raise my hands and *call for the source of all power.*

Wakan-Tanka guide us on this journey.

Let us see through the veils of this earth world into the other worlds that live with this one.

Oh Spirit Wind, let us follow you through the holes and cracks into the unknown.

Slowly the land starts to move and weave into shapes. It seems very strange.

I have never encountered this before in the Ordinary World. It is like there are two pictures merging into each other and pulsating outward. We are in an electromagnetic belt that bridges the Ordinary World with the Unordinary World. The energy starts to become very intense. For a flash, I move into slow motion. I see a pueblo city built on the side of Courthouse Rock. The sound of a low humming vibration from some unknown source brings me back into reality, if there is such a thing at this point.

"There are yellow, violet, red and lavender colors darting around us!" Adele yells out.

I, too, see a foggy mist of yellow light with a violet tint glow in translucent form. Slowly everything around me is fluid and in a million atoms. I feel myself flowing toward Courthouse Rock.

I am moving through a long tunnel corridor that seems man-made. I can see Adele and Susie walking hand in hand next to me. Round translucent balls of blue light hang motionlessly in suspended animation. I ask Adele what she is seeing.

"I am in a long tunnel with you and Susie and I see round globes sending out blue light."

I don't know if I am speaking to her vocally or telepathically. I do know we're communicating and all together. We enter a large square room, two stories tall. I see a table.

"Do you see a table?" I ask Adele.

"Yes," she says. Then she starts to describe it. "It is a long table with a white cloth. Its edges hang over the sides."

From now on the three of us see and experience the same things, though at the time we were not fully cognizant of this. Only later that evening, after we talked, did we recall the same details.

I can see a group of people clustered in the shadows of the room. We had been told by Anton that there would be over twenty present and awaiting our arrival.

"You have entered a Holy Sanctuary." A deep sounding voice from out of the shadows speaks. "*From ancient times this has been a Lemurian Sacred Temple.* This temple is connected to many other underground mountain centers by corridors deep within the earth."

The person speaking moves out of the shadows and continues. He is a thin man at least seven feet tall with long blond hair. He is dressed in a long white gown with gold sandals. His bright blue eyes shimmer.

"I am Kaleaf. In this land and vortex you call Sedona we welcome you to our Sacred Temple. You David, come as a Joiner to bring Adele and Susie to us. I promise you will not go away empty-handed. There is a gift for you to receive also."

A woman comes out of the shadows. It is strange yet I know she is a very Holy Woman with great heavenly and earthly powers. She is dressed in a long white gown and blue cape. An aura of gold glows around her body.

Adele kneels before her and tears of love stream from Adele's eyes. She looks up toward this holy woman's face that is radiant with love and compassion. Though I am standing quite a distance away I can feel that she is an Earth Mother and loves her Earth Children.

"I came to you when you were a child of five."

"Are you *Mother Mary?*" Adele asks in a soft voice.

"Yes! I am the *mother of Sananda.*"

The name Sananda is the spacehood's name for Jesus. In ancient Indian lore Jesus visited the American Indian Nation after his resurrection.

Her voice is flowing. "We met in another lifetime when you were a *disciple of my Son and a member of the Christ Family.* You came into this life experience as a *walk-in.* You don't remember that part of your life but you do remember that you entered. You saw me dressed as I am now in white gown and blue cape, giving you water.

Driving home later, Adele told me when she was a child, she awoke to see a woman in white with a blue cape giving her water out of a silver goblet. She knew it was Mother Mary but felt that most people could not understand her experience and would ridicule her. The only other person to know of this experience was her mother but she thought it was a child's hallucination.

The Mother of Sananda goes on, "I came to you when you entered in as a walk-in and had you drink of the Holy water so you would retain your past spiritual growth."

Everything starts to weave and move into fluid shapes and I am sucked out of the mountain at a tremendous speed. I am sitting in the same spot. I am in some form of suspended animation. I see the land and mountain move in waves of electro-magnetism. For the first time I am conscious that I am standing in the doorway between the Ordinary and Nonordinary World. Then the misty-ice within the cube I am sitting in starts pulsating. I watch Adele and Susie *kneeling before Sananda*. His voice is very soft and a tremendous aura glows around his body. The whole room is silent but for Him speaking. The love that pours forth from Sananda makes strong tears flow down my face. This sensation of love seems to center me with the God within. I feel a great peace and truth, a harmony of onement with everything, a center of divine unity. I watch the blessing and it is as if I am looking at a double exposure. I see the time on earth overlaid to this vision.

Sananda speaks, "The children are the lambs of the earth, we must protect them."

"I love you, Sananda," Susie beams.

He reaches down and picks her up.

"My Father in Heaven is saddened that so many children suffer on the Kingdom of Earth while the self-righteous are caught in their self-judgement and no longer talk to My Father."

Sananda sets Susie down.

"Both of you once walked with me when I was embodied in an earth body. Susie walked with me as a child and you Adele, as a faithful disciple. My Mother remembers that you were with me as they nailed me to the cross and you were there at my resurrection. Your faith helped her through the darkness of the night into the light of day. Later, as a member of the Christ Family, you went out to teach and heal."

Sananda's love fills the room, and then He turns slowly and walks away. For a moment it is as if we are terribly alone, isolated from a source so wonderful that it is like leaving the warm womb of our mother and being cast out into the world.

The Initiation continues and Adele sees and talks with her guides Gabriel, Murye from Venus, Matrey of the Center Earth, and Anton, her space brother. Then we see and talk to Star Commander Varcus, as well as my Master who is called the Wise Old One, and North Star, my Lemurian protector. During this time we were given guidance and learning that we would bring back with us.

We become conscious of sitting outside. Tears of emotion run down our faces. We look at each other and through the tears we start laughing. We hug each other and let the strong energy locked within the experience fill us. The stirring wind dries our wet faces.

"It was beautiful!" I gasp. I knew what I felt and saw could never be understood by words alone. It was part of one's private emotion. All of us were bestowed with a wonderful gift that will be part of our eternal experience. Our hearts had been touched by the Divine Force.

"Mommy! Mommy! I saw Jesus!" Her face is bright and smiling. "He held me, Mommy. Did you see him hold me?"

"Oh yes, Darling, Mommy saw him hold you. He loves you very much, as I love you."

Later that night I deliver the following chant, influenced by the vision and our standing on sacred ground.

Oh gentle Spirit Wind that carried us in to the realm of Divine Light, we thank you.

Oh Gentle Spirit Wind that encompassed us with Master Sananda and Mother Mary, we thank you once again.

Each blessing received in Thy Divine House will always be a part of this dedicated space in our own hearts.

We thank each one of you for the gifts you brought us.

I bless this land, the Four Sacred Corners.

I thank the Guardian Protectors for letting us in.

The Grandmothers and Grandfathers for their guidance.

Father Sun and Mother Moon for their direction.

I thank the White Buffalo Spirit for its presence.

I thank the wolf who built the trails upon the earth.

Oh Great White Father, hear our thanks and gratitude.

Slowly we move down the hill to where the jeep is parked and drive to the motel.

After the three of us wash up, we drive to a restaurant for dinner. We talk about the initiation and the strange but beautiful encounters we all shared. Adele suggests we go toward the mountains and see if we can see a Space Craft. We park the jeep on a dark street. Since it is rattlesnake time we all sit on the hood. At this time of night the snakes come to the lawns in front of houses for water.

I am gazing upward. We see several lights moving in patterns identical to space craft. Then all of a sudden *a rainbow of light flashes across the sky*. It had to be a small craft because it maneuvered like a jet fighter, rolling, diving, and then looping.

"*A rainbow,*" Susie yells. "I saw a rainbow!"

"Darn it, I didn't see it," Adele says. "Did you see it, David?"

"Yes. Its motors gave off a rainbow effect. It was beautiful."

Fog comes in quickly.

"Well, we might as well go back to the motel . . . the fog is coming in." Adele says.

We all get ready for bed and turn in. Once the lights are turned off I can see misty yellow-violet colors in the room. Everything still seems to be moving in and out of another dimension.

"We're still not fully back, Adele. We're moving in and out of an electromagnetic wave."

"I know. It is so strange, David."

I let myself flow with the energy. Susie has fallen asleep and Adele is just about to. There would be no other day like this one, yet there would be other days because the door was open.

Sedona is a "special" location in the heart of Indian land which all truth seekers should journey to sometime in their life.

Publishers note: The above is excerpted from the book *Lemurian Atlantean Vision Wheel* which may be ordered from Lost World Publishing, Suite #381, 2899 Agoura Rd., Westlake Village, CA 91361

Celebrate The Legendary Ways of the Shamans

and Experience the Supernatural Powers of Native Indian Prophecy, Mysticism & Spirituality

Here are four remarkable works and one audio cassette tape that will lead you on a personal vision quest. Find out why thousands of metaphysical students are turning to the "Good Red Road" and the ways of the medicine men and tribal chiefs for inner perfection and personal guidance.

#1—New December 1991
MYSTICAL LEGENDS OF THE SHAMANS
by Brad and Sherry Steiger

Here are the little known legends involving the spiritual and mystical as well as psychic experiences of the North American Indians—the medicine men, chiefs and shamans of various tribes. A rare collection of Amerindian legends that have been repeated by generations of shamans employing the oral tradition of telling enchanting tales around the evening campfires. The incredible power of these legends remains undimmed by the passage of time, and their applications of vital truths for modern men and women becoming increasingly self-evident. Among the mystic shamanistic legends are such tales as: • How the spirits of the four winds came to be. • When the animals ruled the Earth mother. • The origin of the races. • The first battle between good and evil. • Entering the land of shadows. • Mysterious visitors to our world. • The ghostly canoe. • The daughter of the evening star descends to take a husband • Spirit beings of thunder and lightning, and many, many more.

There is also a special section: STARS: GUARDIANS OF THE NIGHT—on Amerindian cosmology; revelations of things to come in the chapter, THE EARTH MOTHER AND PROPHECY; sacred talismans that can be put to personal work for you in the section AMERICAN INDIAN POWER SYMBOLS, and finally a timely photographic portfolio of the great medicine men and chiefs of our time.

This beautiful, coffee table-sized book, contains 100 pages and comes complete with a glorious air-brushed cover painted by native American artist Timoteo Ikoshy Montoya. To order simply circle #1 in the order coupon—$12.95.

#2—New December 1991
THE AMERICAN INDIAN UFO-STARSEED CONNECTION
Edited and annotated by Timothy Green Beckley

Do the various Amerindian tribes know a lot more about space visitors than the rest of us—including, perhaps, even the United States government?

With chapters by some of the most astute metaphysical writers, such as Brad Steiger, Diane Tessman, David Jungclause and Chris Franz, this book delves into the traumatic "Last Days" that many sensitives say are not far off and the "feeling" that the Indians may help lead us to a safe New World based upon their connection with beings from other realms and worlds.

Explored are striking revelations concerning the famous Hopi Prophecies and a mysterious artifact unearthed at the site of a newly discovered pyramid that suggests that the end of the current cycle of Mother Earth is about to come to an end, and that something more "wonderful" will replace it as we are pulled brother with brother toward the climax of an era.

Learn the significance of the Kachina spirits of the sky and when they are to return; what meaning the creature known as Bigfoot has in relationship to the Indian tribes; why UFOs are so frequently seen—even today—over the various reservations. Find out what the mysterious "Star symbol" of the UFO-nauts means in the context of the sacred Medicine Wheel, and how the dreams that many of us are now having may turn out to be very prophetic.

This is a large sized book containing over 100 pages. When released in December it will retail for $14.95. Order now at the special pre-publication price by circling #2 on the order coupon—$12.95.

#3
AMERICAN INDIAN CEREMONIES—
A PRACTICAL GUIDE TO THE MEDICINE PATH
by Medicine Hawk and Gray Cat

Medicine Hawk (Council Chief, the Shadowlight Medicine Clan) and Gray Cat (editor, the *Crone Papers*) present dozens of practical and concise ceremonies enabling the reader to practice the concepts of the Sacred Pipe and the Medicine Wheel, regardless of their heritage and in a manner that is true to the environment of our living Earth.

Learn to master the ancient and sacred ways that can now be passed to the Truth Seeker as we enter a New Age of Spiritual Enlightenment. Here are all the powers and tools YOU will ever need to Walk the Good Red Road.

Discusses in detail the construction of the Medicine Wheel, the true role of the Vision Quest, the use of the Sacred Pipe, the relationship of the Sweat Lodge, the important of the Animal and plant kingdoms, as well as the magick in pictographs and symbols.

This volume contains 150 8½x11 pages and is attractively illustrated with photos, graphs and charts. Circle number 3 on the order form—$14.95.

#4
AMERICAN INDIAN MAGIC—
SACRED POW WOWS & HOPI PROPHECIES
by Brad Steiger

Through a few simple techniques the reader will learn how to make American Indian Magic work for YOU! Over the centuries, the native American priests have practiced a system of magic so powerful that it enables them to control the winds and the weather, to foresee coming events, and sometimes even to change the future. They have always possessed the ability to heal the sick, to walk over burning coals, to read minds, to send and receive telepathic thoughts, to communicate with the dead, speak to animals, and to control others at a distance. This book is a practical guide which teaches, among other things, the American Indian's way to perfection, telling the reader how to: • Hold your own "Vision Quest." • Communicate with spirits and angels and get them to assist you in all that you desire. • Take control of every situation and through a formal agreement with the forces of nature, receive incredible benefits that can turn your life around for the better.

Circle #4 and find out how Indian Magic can be of service to you!—$12.95.

#5
60 MINUTE AUDIO CASSETTE
INDIAN MEDICINE WHEEL
with Brad Steiger

Journey to dimensions never before experienced with this Altered States Awareness cassette tape. Hold your own Vision Quest, prepare your own Medicine Bag of sacred and highly charged objects. Communicate with spirits of the Earth and Sky. Many tribes believe that the Medicine Wheel can cure the sick, ward off evil and bring great blessings. Now the author of **AMERICAN INDIAN MAGIC** leads you through various meditations complete with authentic Indian prayers and chants. Circle number 5 for this outstanding audio cassette tape—$9.95.